The Other Talk

A Boomer's guide to talking with your family about the rest of your life

by
Tim Prosch

ABOUT THIS BOOK

One of the most important conversations you will have with your children is what is euphemistically called the Talk, the one about the birds and the bees. However, there is another equally critical time in your kids' lives when you need to sit them down to talk about the facts of life.

It's the Other Talk. This time it's not about the beginning of life. It's about your last chapter of life and the issues and decisions and role reversals that you and your family need to confront while you are still able to lead the conversation.

The Other Talk is designed to help you get past the many emotional barriers to an open, honest dialogue and to guide you into a thorough discussion of the four facts of life:

1. Financing your uncertain future

2. Selecting the most effective living arrangement

3. Getting the medical care you need

4. Taking charge at the end of your life

Start reading this book today so you can begin preparing for one of the most important conversations your family will ever have.

TABLE OF CONTENTS

Appendix

INTRODUCTION

In today's book environment, whether it be on actual or virtual shelves, you'll find many titles that provide tips and techniques on how to care for and cope with an aging and ultimately dying parent.

Typically, these self-help books are designed to assist adult children who have been confronted by any one of a number of unexpected crises that disrupt their parents' lives:

- Physical: broken hip, diagnosis of life-threatening illness

- Financial: sudden spike in medical expenses, unexpected decline in net worth

- Psychological: emergence of mental illness, onslaught of dementia

The problem is that these books focus on what to do *after* a parent care crisis hits. While this reactive approach is necessary in coping with the challenges that occur in front of you, it is built on the assumption that the crisis is the children's cross to bear, and that the parents have become innocent bystanders. Further, this problem/solution mind-set ignores the long-term emotional consequences that can subvert both sides of the family relationship:

- the children can become overwhelmed by the depth and breadth of responsibilities and the emotional stress of guessing, and being second-guessed on, what the parents would want done in a given situation

- the last years of the aging parents can be made miserable by the resentments associated with their loss of control over day-to-day living and the feelings of embarrassment and failure at becoming a "burden to the kids"

Preempting the Crisis

The Other Talk takes the polar opposite approach from all those "coping with a failing, incompetent parent" volumes.

First, it places the responsibility for taking action directly in the hands of the parents, not the kids. By adopting this preemptive, collaborative mind-set, the parents will actually empower every member of their family (themselves as well as their children) for the events that lie ahead.

Second, it takes a proactive approach by helping the reader prepare for various decisions and actions that need to be taken throughout the last chapter of life, rather than waiting for the next unexpected (although often predictable) crisis to envelop the family.

Clearly, no one knows how the last sentence of one's life will be written . . . how and when declining health and death will occur. But we all know with a fair amount of certainty what issues will arise, and the decisions that will need to be made in our last chapter of life.

I believe the answer is that parents need to take the initiative to have what I call the Other Talk with their kids. They need to sit the family down and walk through the four facts of life in the last chapter of life while they are still physically and mentally able to lead that discussion.

1. Financing your uncertain future (How do you budget for unknown needs and an uncertain length of time?)

2. Selecting the most effective living arrangement (If and when do you move to an assisted-living facility?)

3. Getting the medical care you need (Who will advocate for your medical needs, and how?)

4. Taking charge at the end of life (How do you want your kids to start taking over decision making when you no longer can?)

Of course, the ultimate goal here is to provide you with the tools and the road map to successfully engage your own kids in the Other Talk:

1. First, by overcoming the emotional hurdles that will present themselves when you address your eventual demise and explore the role reversal that you and your kids will experience

2. Second, by providing concepts and techniques that will help you and your family thoroughly understand and prepare for the facts of life in your last chapter of life

What Drove Me to Write This Book?

Throughout my career as a brand manager, I have focused my energies and attention on understanding and addressing the needs, wants, and challenges of the Baby Boom generation for a variety of national and international organizations.

For the past fifteen years running a strategic marketing consultancy, I have homed in on elder care and end-of-life issues.

That experience, combined with four specific events, drove me to write this book.

1. Over the last ten years, I have been interviewing hundreds of Baby Boomers to determine the perceptions, attitudes, and mind-set that this unique generation brings to the various decisions at the end of life. One clear message was that Baby Boomers do not want their kids to suffer through the same

frustrations, arguments, and unpleasant surprises that they themselves experienced with their parents.

2. In 2005, the Terri Schiavo case captured the attention (and heart strings) of the world, especially the tug-of-war between Terri's husband and her parents over what she wanted done at the end of her life.

3. Concurrently, over the last four years, I have experienced, through the rapidly declining health of my own parents, the escalating frustrations and financial crises that lack of communication can create.

4. For Baby Boomers, there is a "Perfect Storm" that has been brewing in geriatric care in recent years, and it's scheduled to hit the Boomers just as they reach sixty-five:

   - More: The sixty-five-and-older population will grow more than 60 percent between now and 2025

   - Longer: Today's sixty-five-year-old will likely live for another 18.5 years

   - Fewer: The supply of geriatric doctors and nurses is declining

Boomers and their kids need to start preparing. They should have the Other Talk now; then keep on talking.

This book is the catalyst that can get you there!

THE OTHER TALK

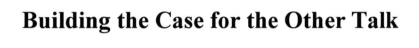

Building the Case for the Other Talk

CHAPTER ONE

DEFINING THE DIMENSIONS OF THE OTHER TALK

Do you remember how difficult—and absolutely necessary—it was when it came time to sit with your kids to have "the Talk," the one about the birds and the bees? If you are anything like me, your initial reaction was to procrastinate, to keep the door firmly closed on any conversations that revolved around orgasms and vaginas and penises with your twelve-year-old (in my case, daughter).

But why would I even consider putting off a conversation that was so critical to the future well-being of my child?

1. Emotionally challenging subject

First of all, it was uncomfortable and embarrassing to sit down with my daughter to explain how the body parts interact and what the physical sensations would be.

2. Denial of inevitable changes

Second, if we didn't have the Talk, I could hold on just a little longer to my fantasy that my little girl, my bouncy, energetic, wide-eyed, giggly preteen, would remain just that . . . forever.

3. Evolution of parent/child interaction

In addition, I could continue to pretend that our relationship would never change. We'd still read the Sunday comics on the couch, I'd still help her with her homework, and I wouldn't have to contemplate some boy mauling her in the backseat of his car (or, God forbid, vice versa).

4. The value of stepping up

Because of the expected discomfort both for me and my daughter, I even contemplated the sex-talk drive-by, where I would drop off the brochures on her bed with the note, "Let me know if you have any questions." As a result, I could stay hidden behind the birds-and-the-bees euphemism and avoid any real semblance of a two-way dialogue.

But, of course, the Talk isn't just about plumbing issues, like where things go, how things work, and how embryos turn into babies. It's also about the judgments and decisions that need to be made as our children enter an important new chapter in their lives.

Ultimately, I confronted my procrastination and stepped up to the Talk, because I recognized that there were real, life-altering consequences to putting it off indefinitely: possible unexpected pregnancy, sexual disease, and unfulfilling relationships with the opposite sex, to name a few.

Initially, the Talk was uncomfortable for both my daughter and me, but, as the first conversation unfolded and subsequent ones ensued, we both began to realize that we were empowering her for something that would have far-reaching and ongoing consequences for the rest of her life.

The Other Talk

There is another equally critical time in your kids' lives when you need to sit them down to talk about the facts of life. This time it's not about the beginning of life or how babies are made. It's about the end of life—yours—and the many issues and decisions that will confront you and your children during your last chapter of life (some call it the retirement years).

It's the Other Talk.

Unfortunately, if you're anything like the hundreds of families and medical/end-of-life practitioners whom I interviewed in preparation for this book, you will most likely put off indefinitely any substantive discussion with your kids about what they might expect in your last chapter.

In fact, most parents *never* have the Other Talk. Data from the National Hospice Foundation reports that 75 percent of Americans have not made their end-of-life decisions known, through either verbal or written communication.

Furthermore, a recent survey by the AARP found that nearly 70 percent of adult children have not talked to their parents about issues related to aging. Some of them avoid this most intimate of conversations because they believe their parents don't want to talk about it. Others think they know what their parents want. And some simply don't want to face the very real truth that old age will most likely include disease, injury, frailty, even loneliness and depression.

Why do most Americans keep the door firmly closed on the Other Talk? It turns out the thought process is remarkably similar to those that stand in the way of the "birds and the bees" talk.

1. Emotionally challenging subject

First of all, sitting down with your kids to talk about your last chapter can be uncomfortable, painful, depressing, even paralyzing, especially when you come to the part about the various stages of your deterioration, mentally and physically, and, of course, that last sentence:

The end.

I found that to avoid stirring up these scary emotions, many of the parents I interviewed for this book would take a protective stance:

I don't want to put my family in a state of depression and panic by talking about it.

Not surprisingly, the reality is that this sweep-it-under-the-rug attitude usually has as much to do with the mental fragility of the parent as it does with that of the children. It seems the longer we can cling to the previous chapter of our lives (the one where we are healthy, independent, and carefree), the less we need to deal with the final one.

The unfortunate consequence of protecting your kids is that, when circumstances eventually force your family to confront reality, whether it be a serious injury, a severe financial setback, or a life-threatening diagnosis, you (but most likely your kids) will be reacting in crisis mode. As a consequence, your options will most likely be dramatically restricted, and the pressure to make decisions quickly can become overwhelming.

2. Denial of the inevitable changes

Second, the last chapter of life can be a joyous time. You're freed from the constrictions and boundaries of the workaday world. You may be blessed with grandchildren, which offers another form of liberation (e.g., "What happens at Grandma's, stays at Grandma's"). And you have the opportunity to explore new corners of life that you could never find the time for in your younger years.

Because the good parts of the last chapter of life are so enjoyable, almost everyone I interviewed wanted to hold on to them for as long as possible by walling off the bad parts. The tool of choice was simple procrastination:

I'm not going to involve my kids in the issues surrounding my end of life until the time is right!

Of course, the time is never right—until it's too late. Often what happens is that the parent is suddenly stricken, mentally or physically—by dementia, heart attack, or fast-moving disease—and, as a consequence, is unable to communicate coherently and effectively on the many decisions that need to be made.

The resulting emotional price that the children will pay for their parents' terminal procrastination will be multidimensional, and, in many cases, will last a lifetime:

- Guilt and feelings of inadequacy over the potentially adverse consequences of their decision making, especially when confronting conflicting opinions from various medical and legal professionals

- Shock over the difficulty of navigating the labyrinth of geriatric medicine

- Helplessness in dealing with the financial destruction created by the cost of geriatric care; in fact, one-third of all personal bankruptcies in America are a direct result of health care expenses, especially in the last eighteen months of life

- Long-term resentment among family members over the wisdom and consequences of decisions made on behalf of the parents in their last chapter of life

3. Evolution of parent/child interaction

Finally, for many of us, the most challenging and sensitive issue that we will come up against in the Other Talk is the changes that we will experience in our last chapter of life.

I'm not referring to the evolving physical condition that we notice as we get older:

- Stamina gets shorter

- Recovery time takes longer

- Morning stiffness is part of waking up

- The row of plastic pill bottles gets longer

- Looking for your reading glasses becomes an hourly event

- Wondering why you just walked into a particular room becomes a regular occurrence

All of this can be mildly annoying, but none of it is debilitating.

But there is a much more fundamental and potentially difficult adjustment that occurs as we enter our last chapter of life, as I learned from the hundreds of interviews I conducted with doctors, nurses, and hospice workers, as well as families: It is the reversal of roles between parent and child that is triggered when you reach the point, physically and/or mentally, where you can no longer operate independently.

In essence, you become the child and your child becomes the parent.

Why is this reversal of roles so difficult and potentially life-changing for both parties? Because it is not merely a mechanical reassignment of responsibilities; it is the shattering of the relationship that you as a parent have had with your children since the day of their birth. As a result, you lose the power and control of being the adult, and your kids give up the security and freedom of being the child.

The Impact of Role Reversal on the Parent

For the parent, the hardest part of growing older may be the crushing realization that

I'm about to lose control of the life and lifestyle that I've worked so hard to create for myself and my spouse.

Despite all the successes you may have achieved throughout life, all the good deeds bestowed on others, all the love and support heaped on family and friends, the great injustice at the end of life is the fear of losing control.

As described by Kathleen, one of my interviewees, it can start out as an uneasy premonition:

Doing it our way isn't going to work indefinitely; in fact, I feel we're in this in-between stage, a time when we can still control how we live but not how much longer we're going to last or be able to make choices before we've become "too old."

When I contemplate it, what we're really dealing with is, "How much longer can we continue to be us?"

Based on my research, I learned that the primary reason that the elderly begin to actively resist turning over responsibility and decision making to their offspring is their escalating fear of:

- powerlessness

- becoming a burden on the family, physically and financially

- loss of self-worth, self-respect, and dignity

- abandonment by the family

To make matters worse, since most people wait until a crisis hits before confronting the need to transfer power and control to the kids, role reversal is often forced on the parents with little or no discussion.

The Impact of Role Reversal on the Child

For the child, the hardest part of seeing your parents age is the sinking feeling that

I need to start taking responsibility for my parents' lives physically, financially, and socially.

Typically for the kids, the shock of responsibility at the "moment of truth" is followed by feelings of inadequacy, embarrassment, and resentment as the plight of their parents comes to dominate their lives. This cauldron of emotional reactions is hardly surprising, since, for the child who is about to morph into the "parent," there is little training and often no warning that it's time to step into the caregiving role.

Unlike another major occurrence in life, childbirth, there are no prenatal classes on caregiving issues and techniques; there are no showers to help with the expense of the caregiving responsibility—and there's no parent to turn to for advice or just a shoulder to cry on.

As a result, for the child with parental responsibility, the world of role reversal can be a very dark and lonely place. Again, the comparison with childbirth is instructive:

> With child care, there are nine months to prepare; the evolution to term is usually predictable and straightforward; and there is generally a crowding around of family and friends to share in the event.

> With parent care, the catalyst is often a sudden, unexpected crisis; the decline is unpredictable and full of unpleasant surprises; and there is almost never any crowding around of family and friends to share in the event.

Bottom line, the impact of the role-reversal process can be very debilitating for both parent and child. Here's how Ralph, one of my research respondents, described the evolution:

> *When we're kids, we don't think our parents know anything. When we grow up and have our own kids, we realize how smart our parents were.*

> *Then, when our parents are in a position either physically or mentally where they can't fend for themselves, we become their parent. They realize they've lost control.*

> *It's very scary; it's very hard; it's like a punch to the gut for them: "I'm not worth what I used to be."*

> *They go through all that; then you say, "Would you like to move to a nursing home?"*

4. The value of stepping up

I must admit that my first inclination in considering my responsibilities to my daughter in the last chapter of my life was to perform another "drive-by" similar to the birds-and-the-bees/sex books on the bed and the "any questions?" approach. Only this time it would be instructions on how to access the key to the safety-deposit box, which contains a will, a life insurance policy, and a paid-up funeral service receipt.

Fortunately, having heard from my research respondents about the unintended consequences of the "good-bye drive-by," I realized that the Other Talk shouldn't just be about the necessary transactions at the end of life.

It should go beyond funeral and burial plans, wills, and donations to science. It needs to delve into the judgments and decisions that must be made throughout your last chapter, and how your children will both impact and be affected by them.

In essence, the Other Talk covers your entire last chapter, which opens on day one of your retirement. This will require some work on your part, both emotionally and rationally, but ultimately will have powerful implications for your family's remaining time together.

The preparation begins with creating in yourself, then sharing with your kids, a tone and attitude that should permeate the Other Talk:

1. You, the parent, are proactively taking the responsibility for empowering and preparing your kids for the reversal of roles that *will* take place in your last chapter

2. You, the parent, embrace the eventual reversal of roles not as giving up power and control, but rather as achieving security and freedom

It then turns to building a mental framework that will allow a smooth transition when the time comes to shift decision-making responsibilities:

1. First, acknowledging the inevitability of the need for and the wisdom of transferring decision making and management of the day-to-day responsibilities

2. Second, discussing and establishing ground rules on the potential circumstances or triggers that effect the change of responsibilities for key functions such as bill paying, driving, living arrangements, money and asset management, and medical decisions

Finally, the Other Talk culminates in a series of conversations that cover in-depth how you would like to deal with four facts of life in your last chapter:

- Financing your uncertain future

- Selecting the most effective living arrangement

- Getting the medical care you need

- Taking charge at the end of your life

Initially, the Other Talk may be uncomfortable for both you and your children, but as the first conversation unfolds and subsequent ones ensue, you and your family will begin to realize that you are empowering your kids for something that will have far-reaching and ongoing consequences for the rest of their lives.

In essence, the Other Talk can have a powerful impact on your children on a number of levels:

1. Helping them cope with and successfully handle some of the difficult challenges that lie ahead for all of you

2. Creating a new dimension to the family relationship that comes from participating in, rather than suffering through, your last chapter

3. Teaching them how to prepare for their own last chapter

4. Giving your children a thorough understanding and actual experience for when they sit down with their own kids to have the Other Talk

If you are still feeling hesitant or uneasy or unconvinced about having the Other Talk with your family, I would ask you to consider three questions which are addressed in the next three chapters:

1. What will happen if you don't have the Other Talk?

2. What can happen if you do have the Other Talk?

3. How can the Other Talk meet the unique challenges of Baby Boomers' final years?

CHAPTER TWO

RECOGNIZING THE DESTRUCTIVE CONSEQUENCES OF STOIC SILENCE

My great-grandfather had a great life and a perfect ending.

Grandpa emigrated from Germany in his early thirties and, after working hard to learn English, used his considerable woodworking skills to become a master carpenter. While he was often involved in building houses, he was best-known for creating simple but elegant dining room tables and chairs.

When I got to know him, he was pushing ninety, living with his daughter and her husband (my grandparents), but still able to get around enough to tend to his rose garden.

One thing I really looked forward to was going over to watch the Chicago Cubs game with him. Since they often lost (and if Grandma wasn't around), he'd cuss them out pretty good. Ahh, my first taste of male bonding at age eight!

One day in September we watched the Cubs win one and

celebrated with a bowl of butter pecan ice cream (his favorite). Mom came to pick me up, and Gramps headed outside to his rose garden and eventually dozed off. On this particular warm Indian summer afternoon, he didn't wake up.

Quick, painless, uncomplicated, in a place of his choosing, in a final moment of beauty and serenity.

No muss, no fuss, with a Cubs victory to send him on his way.

The Power of Procrastination and Inertia

Grandpa's demise came to be known in our family as the "rose garden exit strategy." Unfortunately, while this story was mildly amusing and, in some ways, comforting, over the years my parents began to firmly (wishfully?) embrace this fantasy of the end of life as their own.

As a result, this mind-set allowed them to sweep all the challenges and unpleasantries of old age and especially death under the rug. If the subject ever came up with me or my two brothers, Mom and Dad's pat answer was always, "Everything will turn out just fine, so we don't need to talk about it."

What I was to learn when I began my research for this book was that the vast majority of parents turn to that same stoic silence whenever confronted with issues or even questions about the last chapter of life.

Based on hundreds of conversations with families and elder care/end-of-life practitioners, a pattern emerged as to how the natural decline of the parents can unleash serious unwanted strains on the entire family relationship. To demonstrate how these unintended consequences of "stoic silence" play out, I will share with you my own family's story.

1. The start down the slippery slope

When my parents reached their late sixties, they decided to sell their home-health-care business and finally retire to their house in the woods overlooking Lake Michigan. Then, to escape Michigan's harsh, gray winters, they transformed themselves into "snowbirds," buying a home near Phoenix.

For the first couple years of retirement, life was great. Many of Mom and Dad's friends from the Midwest had also decided to winter in Phoenix, so there was a ready and comfortable group for them to tap into for trips into the desert and up the mountains, as well as cocktail hour at the end of the day. In addition, the recreation center down the street housed a pottery class and a garden club for Mom, and an outdoor swimming pool and woodworking shop for Dad.

My brothers and I and our wives and kids would go visit, typically in February, and everybody in the family felt that our parents' living arrangement seemed very workable. Dad had been diagnosed with multiple sclerosis twenty years earlier, but was still getting around on a cane and was able to drive. Mom was as energetic and physically fit as she had always been, and was able to effectively play the primary caregiver role. Finally, since they had relocated to one of the retirement villages near Phoenix, there were plenty of medical and other support systems at their fingertips.

Then the crisis hit.

For me, it began on a Wednesday in late March. I was just finishing up a presentation of research findings to a group of senior executives in New York when a secretary came into the boardroom from a side door and handed me a note. It read:

> *Your father's refusing to get into the ambulance.*
> *What do you want to do about it?*

To say I was caught unaware would be an understatement. I looked up at the secretary and indicated that I'd be right there. Once I reached the phone, the crisis began to take shape.

The paramedic indicated that my father had taken a bad fall on the ceramic tile floor in their Spanish-influenced home and likely had fractured his hip, but was refusing to go to the hospital. He also described my mother's condition as frightened and incoherent, not surprising under the circumstances, but also not her usual cool, calm, take-charge self.

Fortunately, my brother Doug had planned a trip out to Phoenix with his family and was, in fact, scheduled to arrive the next day. Unable to communicate with Mom, I got Dad on the phone and convinced him that the emergency room was the best place for him to be. Then I hung up the phone and called Doug to forewarn him that his trip out west was not going to be the usual visit.

Doug called me the next afternoon to describe a situation much worse than any of us had imagined. Dad had also fallen at least three other times in the preceding two weeks. Since Mom, at five-foot-three and 105 pounds, couldn't lift what essentially was deadweight, they called on their neighbor Bill to help get him back up, and swore him to secrecy from the family with, "We don't want to worry them."

Then Doug discovered that the entire right side of my parents' Oldsmobile minivan was smashed in, the result of an accident Mom had had in a parking lot three weeks earlier.

Perhaps most depressing, my brother learned from our parents' doctor that Mom had been diagnosed with Alzheimer's, a horrendous disease that essentially peels away the brain one layer at a time while leaving the body intact. Dad apparently was going to tell us when they returned to Michigan the next summer.

I hung up the phone and felt a cold, numbing sensation of helplessness. As the afternoon turned into evening, the implications for me, my two brothers, and our families really began to sink in with a vengeance.

2. The chilling reality of role reversal

A parent care crisis is particularly devastating, because reality hits you from two sides.

Reality number one for me and my two brothers was our total shock over our parents' deteriorated condition.

- Dad's MS had finally won the battle with his ability to walk, so that he would be forever confined to a wheelchair. Equally disturbing, his disease had begun to aggressively attack his cognitive functions, particularly his short-term memory, organizational skills, and attention span

- Mom's Alzheimer's was rapidly stealing her ability to communicate. Within three months, she would never utter another coherent sentence for the rest of her life

While their crisis was sudden, their demise would be gradual.

- Mom would live another five years, although in an inchoate and increasingly frightened and antagonistic condition

- Dad would see another seven years, although in a world that swirled with conspiracies and hallucinations

Reality number two was the sinking realization that Doug, Tom, and I, as well as our spouses, would be forced into the parental role with no planning, no expertise, inadequate resources, and, most important, no direction from our parents.

- We discovered that Dad had an investment portfolio that would cover the cost of a stable, healthy retirement scenario, but he had neglected to buy long-term-care insurance to pay for the expense of an extended physical decline of undetermined length.

- We were forced to quickly confront a series of complex and complicated decisions in the areas of:

  a. Financial planning and management

  b. Alternative living arrangements

  c. Medical care for our parents' declining medical conditions

  d. Decision making at the very end of their lives

To make this situation even more overwhelming, the three of us had never discussed any of these issues with our parents, and due to Dad's declining cognitive skills and Mom's increasing incoherence, we never would. As a result, we were literally sailing into uncharted waters without a compass.

3. The challenges lurking in uncharted waters

Clearly, Mom and Dad couldn't live on their own. But it was also obvious that we couldn't expect a logical, well-thought-out answer as to where they'd like to live, so we fell back on the only experience we'd had with a relative needing assisted living, which was Mom's mother.

a. Taking the initiative to establish new directions while you're still able

At age eighty, our grandmother decided to sell her two-story flat, where she had lived upstairs and rented out the lower floor. She was beginning to have trouble navigating the steps and had clearly grown weary of getting the house painted; lining up plumbers, electricians, and yard maintenance; and dealing with renters.

So Grandma moved into an assisted-living senior center, where she had her own apartment, several dining rooms to choose from, a wide variety of social activities, and an extensive travel program that had her visiting someplace new every four months. In addition, there was an on-site advanced-care facility that she could turn to whenever her health required it.

At her ninetieth birthday party, she leaned over to me at dinner and confided, "I've just had the best ten years of my life. You should try it!"

b. Suffering through trial and error in the middle of a

crisis

So the decision on what to do with Mom and Dad seemed obvious: Find a place that could replicate Grandma's experience (Doug offered to take that on in St. Louis, where he lived) and we would be finished.

The signs that this would be an unmitigated disaster began to crop up in the first month.

- Mom refused to leave their apartment except for meals with Dad

- Dad started getting increasingly aggressive and argumentative with the staff

It only got worse a few months into their stay in St. Louis, when Dad (against doctor's orders) escaped to a college reunion in Ohio with the help of two fraternity brothers. Of course, he didn't tell anyone he was going, which after twenty-four hours resulted in panicky phone calls from the assisted-living facility as to his whereabouts, and an escalating frenzy by my late-stage-Alzheimer's mother, who was apparently feeling abandoned in a sea of strangers.

Desperate for a solution, I convened my two brothers and our wives to come up with a plan B, knowing that we couldn't expect any guidance from our parents in their current mental condition.

It finally dawned on us that our parents had always been a very sociable couple, and that many of their friends from the garden club and from their church still resided in their small town in Michigan. When we offered to move them back home, their beaming faces and excited body language told us that we were onto something.

But this path was also fraught with risk. We would need to create a reliable assisted-living support system—medically, physically, financially, and socially—in the middle of the woods, miles from their small downtown and nearly an hour from a hospital, with me in Chicago, Tom in D.C., and Doug in St. Louis.

The learning curve was steep, and the time to execute was short, and along the way we hit many dead ends, wrong turns, and near disasters. Ultimately, keeping them in their home for their entire last chapter turned out to be the right thing. But that journey would have been so much easier, more direct, and less gut-wrenching if we'd had a road map for where to go, and the time to chart how to get there.

Having the Other Talk would have provided us with just the tools we needed.

4. The battle lines in the last chapter of life

As we would soon learn, the initial shock of reversing roles with our parents was only the beginning. Putting their full faith and confidence in a rose garden exit, Mom and Dad would cause a series of unexpected skirmishes between themselves and us that took a heavy emotional toll.

The "Cadillac Moment"

Dad had always been self-sufficient, a take-charge kind of guy; he had to be as a business owner. But in his later years, when his bills started getting paid sporadically and he began running a hundred dollars of overdraft fees every month, I was forced to step in to take over the finances and what little nest egg was left. Not surprisingly, this set off a tug-of-war between the two of us that ran right up to his dying day.

However, this battle for control wouldn't affect just me. I recall what my brothers and I call the "Cadillac moment" that crystallized how difficult the road ahead would be for all of us.

While Dad had apparently lost touch with the reality of money management, he was nothing if not stubborn and resourceful. I remember one weekend my wife Pam and I made the four-hour drive from Chicago to visit the folks. As I pulled into the driveway and opened the garage door, I saw my parents' van was gone. In its place sat a new Cadillac Eldorado.

When we got in the house, my first question was, "Dad, where's the van?"

"I traded it in for the Cadillac. I figured your mom and I

deserved a little splurge," he replied with a sly, satisfied look on his face.

"But what did you use for money?" I asked incredulously.

"I cashed in the CDs at the bank."

As I sank deeper into the old overstuffed couch in the living room, I realized that the loss of the $75,000 in CDs meant that my parents had finally reached insolvency. The sinking continued as it dawned on me that I would now need to inform my two brothers and each of our wives that we were on the hook for whatever expenses Medicare didn't cover. Worse yet, I couldn't tell them how long that financial obligation would last, but I could assure them that the debt was already considerable, due to the large home-equity loan that Dad had taken out years ago to cover their overseas travels.

"Nothing Needs to Change"

My wife, Pam remembers an equally telling anecdote about my mother:

> When Tim and I got married, his mom welcomed me into the family like a long-lost daughter. What I really liked about her was the energy and passion that she brought not only to her family but also to her home.
>
> Then, a couple of years ago, Mom started having accidents in the kitchen. Some of her favorite meals were turning out inedible when she mixed up

ingredients. More and more of her prized antique glassware was getting broken. And when the fire department had to be called because she left stove burners on to go watch TV, Tim and I knew it was time to move his parents to an assisted-living facility.

The movers had come in the day before to pack everything up; I kept Mom occupied with an extended shopping excursion and a long lunch at her favorite restaurant.

When I came downstairs the next morning, I found Mom surrounded by empty boxes marked, "Kitchen stuff." All the contents had been put back in their accustomed places.

As I wended my way amid the boxes and piles of crumpled newspaper, she rose up to her full five feet, three inches and fixed me with an icy stare I had never seen from her before.

"Pamela, dear," she said quietly but firmly, "Dad and I never agreed to move out of here, and that's not going to change. Now help me put this house back in order."

5. The casualties *during* the last chapter

There were a number of mistakes that we as a family stumbled through along the way. But what really hurt was the disintegration of the loving, trusting relationship that had bound the five of us and our extended families together for so many years.

Here's how Tom, the youngest son, saw the crumbling family dynamic.

It seems parents reach a point where they just don't trust anybody. The fear is, "If I give up control, you'll throw me out on the street. You're taking away all this stuff that I've had all my life." To them, it looks like you've gone too far, like you're trying to pull a fast one.

Doug, the middle son, first felt the breakdown of the family relationship when he showed up in Arizona the day after my forewarning phone call.

The moment he arrived at our parents' house, it became clear that their days of living independently in their home were long gone. Our father's mobility had deteriorated to the point that he was permanently relegated to a wheelchair. More ominously for both of them, our mother's Alzheimer's had rendered her dangerous in the kitchen and behind the wheel of her car. The depressing implication of their new reality was that our mother's role as caregiver and, therefore, guarantor of their independent status had come to an end.

I remember sitting with Mom in her kitchen, looking out at her prized grapefruit tree, trying to convince her that everything was going to be all right. As I struggled to come up with the words that would persuade her to give up that grapefruit tree and everything else that went with it so she and Dad could move into assisted living, I realized that we were asking her to stop being an adult.

We were telling her that she and my father were no longer capable of making intelligent decisions, of using good judgment, of managing their own money, of coming and going whenever they pleased, or of living in their own home.

We were telling her that, while she had done a great job of being an adult for the last seventy years, it was now time for her to be six years old again.

Her tears of anger and resentment are an image I'll never be able to shake.

As I was the oldest, my initial reaction was to maintain a laser focus on how to keep things together, wrestling with why and how and who would be responsible for quality of life in my parents' last chapter. Yet ultimately, despite my considerable commitment of time and energy to this effort, my relationship with my proud, often stubborn father spiraled steadily downward.

Every time I was forced to take another step toward role reversal as my parents declined, I could sense from my father's angry words and body language that he saw it all as a conspiracy to steal his dignity.

- When I began to sell his stocks to pay for my parents' major medical bills and living expenses, he saw it as the destruction of his independence.

- When I took over the bill paying to put an end to utility company threats to turn off the heat, lights, and phone, Dad detected a challenge to his manhood.

- When I was forced to invoke health-care power of attorney to allow the ambulance driver to take my mother to the emergency room over my father's objections, he felt a personal affront to his authority.

Somehow I'd become the enemy, the one who was stealing things behind his back, the one who was constantly plotting to make his life miserable.

God, I wish we'd talked about this stuff when things were more normal!

6. The casualties *after* the last chapter

As so often happens to families who try to sweep end-of-life issues under the rug, bad consequences don't end with the death of the parents. The story of Sara, Kate, and Jon, friends of mine since childhood represents the experience of many families I spent time with in preparing to write this book.

My friends' parents hadn't done any real contingency planning for their last chapter, nor shared with their three children how they'd like decisions made when they were physically and mentally capable. As a result, the lives of Sara, Kate, and Jon were tragically altered in ways that their parents certainly didn't intend.

Jon, as the baby in the family, had grown up being taken care of by his two older sisters. So when the responsibilities of role reversal started piling up, he was at a loss as to what to do. Since his parents had created a vacuum for their kids by never having the Other Talk, Jon opted for the sidelines.

Ultimately, he defined his role as critic of his sisters' decision making, usually after the fact, and as a result rarely participated in the care of his parents. And when it became apparent that not only was there no estate left, but there was a rather large debt incurred for medical needs and assisted living, Jon blamed his sisters for this predicament and simply walked away from the family, even though he lived only twenty minutes away from his parents.

Kate, the caregiver of the three, suffered a fate that afflicts many adult children who attempt to deal with their parents' medical and emotional needs from a distance.

Kate's employer, a large advertising agency in Chicago, valued her skill and accomplishments as an art director, and had cut her a good deal of slack to take care of her parents, who lived almost four hours away. But ultimately her drop in productivity collided with the need to perform in high-pressure, short-lead-time situations, and Kate lost her job.

Unfortunately, she has been out of work for almost two years, which has put a severe strain on her family's finances and her relationship with her husband.

Sara, the one who took on the job of keeping the trains running on time, learned the hard way why 30 percent of bankruptcies in America are caused by overwhelming medical bills.

When her father's modest savings were used up, Sara took out a home-equity loan on her house to pay for her parents' expenses. When her father passed away (her mother had died eighteen months earlier), Sara was faced with:

1. a bank loan that had reached 130 percent of the value of her house due to a real estate freefall

2. her formerly lucrative research business that had slowed to a crawl

3. a sister who had committed to help repay the home equity loan . . . but now couldn't

4. a brother who had left the reservation

Sara and her husband lost their house and begrudgingly tried to pick up the pieces after declaring bankruptcy. Ultimately, the situation proved too much for the two of them, ending in divorce.

It is safe to say that their parents didn't intend this outcome for their children.

It is also highly likely that, if the two parents had embraced the concept of the Other Talk rather than desperately clinging to their version of the rose garden exit strategy, Sara, Kate, and Jon would be in a very different place today—emotionally, psychologically, and financially.

The ultimate goal of this book is to help you avoid the destructive consequences of stoic silence by providing you with tools and the road map to successfully engage your own kids in the Other Talk, first by overcoming the emotional hurdles that will present themselves when you , address your eventual demise and explore the role reversal that you and your kids will experience, and second, by providing concepts and techniques that will help you and your family thoroughly understand and prepare for the facts of life in your last chapter of life.

CHAPTER THREE

APPRECIATING THE TWO-WAY BENEFITS
OF FAMILY COLLABORATION

In my hundreds of interviews, I heard a number of tales that mirrored the experiences of Jon, Kate, and Sara, and, of course, my own. While each narrative contained its own unique mix of details, most of my storytellers ended with the same conclusion: "I'll never put my kids through what just happened to me!"

Yet they most likely will, just like the generations before them did, because the prospect of talking about dying and role reversal has a way of freezing even the most resolute from acting on the premise.

I might have followed in their footsteps except for two catalysts that jump started me and my wife, Pam, into action. The first was the Terri Schiavo saga; the second was a nearly "lights-out" experience on a sailboat.

The Terri Schiavo Case

In February of 1990, a young woman named Terri Schiavo suddenly collapsed while at home, suffering an oxygen cutoff from her brain for several minutes. The result was severe brain damage, although she could breathe and maintain a heartbeat on her own. However, she did need a feeding tube connected to her stomach to keep her alive.

The story of her next fifteen years would have a painful, ultimately destructive impact on her family, but would also create profound ethical, philosophical, and emotional implications for the entire country, including me and my wife. In fact, it was the springboard that would set us on a journey that would culminate in our developing the concept of the Other Talk.

While the Terri Schiavo case eventually spiraled into a battle royal between right-to-die and right-to-life partisans, each egged on by self-serving politicians, the crux of the matter boiled down to, What did Terri want done at the end of her life?

According to her husband, Michael Schiavo, Terri would not want to be kept alive by artificial means; he claimed that she had told him, "If I ever have to be a burden to anybody, I don't want to live like that."

"My aim is to carry out Terri's wishes," Michael told a reporter two years into the protracted court proceedings. "If Terri would ever know that I had somebody taking care of her bodily functions, she'd kill us all in a heartbeat. She'd be so angry!"

Terri's parents, Bob and Mary Schindler, passionately called into question Michael's assertions. They maintained that it would be totally out of character for Terri to take such a stance, because she was a devout Roman Catholic who believed in the sanctity of life.

Unfortunately, there was nothing in writing to back up either side's position. Worse yet, Terri was ultimately reduced to a pawn to be fought over by the two warring factions. Her feeding tube was disconnected for three days in April 2001 before a court reversed the order, and again for six days in January 2003, until another legal challenge put her back on.

On March 18, 2005, her feeding tube was removed one more time. She died at a hospice facility in central Florida on March 31.

While none of us will ever know what Terri wanted done at the end of her life, it's safe to say that her on-again, off-again existence, with its corollary of a highly toxic family dynamic, is not what she or anyone else would wish for.

The Beginnings of the Other Talk

Terri's plight and the tearing apart of her family affected millions of people from around the world in a variety of ways. For Pam and me, it led us to sit down with our thirty-four-year-old daughter, Dakota, a Montessori teacher, and her thirty-six-year-old husband, Fernando, a manager of Internet operations, to talk about the implications of the Schiavo case for our family.

Initially, the conversation revolved around the chaos and heartbreak that were generated by the tug-of-war between Terri's husband and her parents. But it would evolve into a deeper discussion of what we as a group could do to avoid the train wreck that had engulfed Terri and her family.

As I had discovered in researching the Schiavo case, there are two legal documents that serve that exact purpose. Taken together the durable powers of attorney for health care and the health care proxy designation allow an individual to appoint someone to make health-care decisions on his or her behalf if that person is incapacitated by a debilitating illness or a serious injury. The four of us agreed that these would be important documents to have—for two reasons:

1. For Pam and me—if one of us were suddenly stricken as Terri was

2. For both Dakota and Fernando—when the two of us reach the point that we are unable physically or mentally to deal with health care decisions

Then the discussion turned to the key issue of the Schiavo case: What did Terri want done at the end of her life? Short of any written instructions from her, Terri's parents and husband spent years fighting over diametrically opposed interpretations of what Terri might have wanted.

As I dug deeper into the advanced-directive world, I discovered that there exists a legal document called a living will that provides instructions on the course of treatment to be followed by health care providers, caregivers, and the health care proxy designee in the event that an individual is unable to make and communicate health care decisions.

Ever the teacher, Dakota suggested that, as a learning exercise, we each think about, then write down, how Pam and I might compose our own personal living wills.

The next week, as the four of us began to share our opinions on the content of the two living wills, we were surprised to discover a variety of interpretations of what Pam or I would want to happen.

- Fernando assumed that I would want to fight until my last dying breath, and that Pam would want things ended if she were put on a feeding tube for more than a week

- Dakota followed the guilt-trip route of keeping us both going by artificial means, in case a cure were somehow discovered

- Pam and I both guessed wrong on the other's wishes, primarily because we had never had nor wanted to have this conversation

We all agreed that we would meet again after Pam and I returned from an upcoming vacation to Italy, to work out more precise interpretations and legal descriptions of our wishes at the end of our lives.

Little did I know that I was headed for an up-close-and-personal interface with the price of leisurely postponement and procrastination.

<u>My Call to Action</u>

The trip was an eight-day bike tour through the lush and hilly countryside of Tuscany. At the end of the cycling excursion, Pam and I headed off for some R & R in Cinque Terre, a collection of wonderfully picturesque villages perched on hills overlooking the Mediterranean Sea. Since no cars are allowed, the only way to travel was on foot, or by ferry or train.

Or to commission a forty-five-foot sailboat, which sounded like great fun, and certainly safe enough, since the vessel came with a skipper and a crew.

The boat was indeed spectacular. The captain and his mates had spent almost a year restoring and refinishing the teak mast, flooring, and a boom that was almost twenty feet long. (More about that boom in a moment.)

When we left the dock, the skipper kept the sails furled and instead used the motor to get from town to town, giving us a running commentary about the beautifully quaint homes that clung to the sides of the cliffs overlooking the sea.

After an hour of this, I started pestering the crew to put up the sails, turn off the engine, and head out into the Mediterranean. They eventually acquiesced.

Twenty minutes into the sail, a sudden strong wind came up, and it quickly dawned on me from the looks of panic on their faces that the crew members were boat refinishers, not boat navigators.

As the only experienced sailor on the boat, I told the skipper to head into the wind and hold it there while I worked with the crew to bring down the sails. Two minutes later, the skipper decided to help with the sails, leaving the tiller unattended, which caused the boat and that twenty-foot teak boom to begin to rock violently from side to side. That's the last image I remember of being on the boat.

My next recollection is of lying on a gurney in a chaotic and fairly rudimentary emergency room. I couldn't move. I couldn't speak. I couldn't even make a sound. But I could think, and what began to roll through my mind was the conversation about end-of-life decisions that Pam and I and the kids had left unfinished until after the bike trip. Would our procrastination mean that we would suffer the same fate as the Schiavo family?

Fortunately I recovered, although it took fifty stitches across the top of my skull, where that teak boom had landed. Needless to say, in light of my brush with paralysis, brain damage, or worse, the family quickly put into writing the directions and thought processes that Pam and I wanted followed when and if it came time to invoke our respective health care documents.

The Evolution of the Other Talk

However, an important epiphany grew out of my encounter with that twenty-foot-long teak boom. In addition to establishing written contingency plans in the form of living wills, as well as health care power of attorney and proxy designations, Pam and I executed wills, took out life insurance policies, and developed a retirement income and spending plan.

Many people would say that these actions constitute the full extent of family planning.

But it dawned on Pam and me that we could do better. We had come to realize that, while we're still physically, mentally, and emotionally sharp, we need to be talking with our kids not just about what to do at the end medically, but also about the challenges, difficult decisions, changing roles, and shifting responsibilities that Dakota and Fernando will undoubtedly be part of between now and then.

We realized that we needed to include in the Other Talk not only decisions at the end, but also a discussion of the facts of life that span the entire last chapter of life, including:

- financing your uncertain future

- selecting the most effective living arrangement

- getting the medical care you need

- taking charge at the end of life

Finally, it struck us that our family plan should also include trigger points for when a particular responsibility needs to shift from parent to child. This is especially important, because the deterioration of cognitive and physical abilities is often gradual, and not as noticeable (or admissible) to the parent as it is to the kids. That's why planning for it has to be done early.

As a result, we developed criteria that we all four could agree to, but that would ultimately empower Dakota and Fernando to make the decision on, say, when, if, and how to change our living arrangement. It will be much better for them, and ultimately for us, if we discuss those decisions now.

Two-way Benefits

By sitting down with Dakota and Fernando to have the Other Talk, Pam and I were not only preparing ourselves and our family for what was to come, but we were also establishing an environment where we could focus much more on all the living that is ahead of us.

In addition, not only has our family gone through a thorough airing of the potential decision points that could emerge in Pam's and my last chapter, but we have also committed for the past three years to reviewing and updating it annually. This "annual checkup" approach benefits both the parents and the kids.

- For Pam and me, it recognizes that our physical and financial condition will likely change in unexpected ways, and our assumptions and beliefs may shift over time

- For Dakota and Fernando, as their own personal, job, and family responsibilities evolve, it allows them to reevaluate and discuss the roles they are able to play in our last chapter

On a more personal level, everybody in the family had his or her own take on how the Other Talk is making an impact on our lives together.

Pam:

What I like about this approach is that it clarifies for me that parenting doesn't end with your kids surviving high school or graduating college or getting married or becoming parents.

It ends with preparing and participating with your children in their role in our last chapter.

In fact, I believe that Tim and I will be making things a little bit easier for Dakota and Fernando as we get older. And hopefully we will show them how to do that for their kids as well.

Dakota:

Dealing with my parents' future before there are panicky late-night phone calls or surprising overdue bills was a gift. I feel prepared, and so do they. Questions I didn't even know I would have to answer have already been thought through by the people it will affect the most.

What the talk taught me, busy with a toddler and not thinking about retirement, was not only how important it is to prepare for my parents' end of life, but also how to model the talk I will have with my son one day.

Fernando:

While the point of the Other Talk was for Pam and Tim to share with us how they wanted to approach their last chapter, it also gave Dakota and me a chance to reflect on how their choices might impact us.

In addition, it helped prepare us for becoming Dakota's parents' "parents" without the typical drama and bad feelings that I've seen in other families.

Finally, it got me thinking about how to broach the subject of the Other Talk with my own parents.

CHAPTER FOUR

NAVIGATING THE BOOMERS' PERFECT STORM

If you've read this far, I'm hoping you are becoming intrigued with what having the Other Talk can offer you and your family:

- a chance to discuss with your kids the various issues and options that arise in the last chapter of life

- an opportunity to create a road map for decision making during the inevitable role reversal that will occur as you get older

- an occasion for you to teach, probe, think about, and share ideas with your kids about the end of life— not only dying, but also coping with the aging process

And if you are a Baby Boomer, the Other Talk you have will be uniquely your own, because you will experience your retirement years in ways previous generations never did, as you have with every other stage of life.

The good news, of course, is that the Boomers will be able to enjoy a longer, healthier, more active lifestyle in their last chapter. And with the unprecedented wealth accumulation piled up by this generation, they can expect to have a whole lot more fun.

However, the flip side of these happy circumstances is what makes the Other Talk not just an opportunity to bond with your kids, but also an imperative if you are to have any hope of managing the rest of your life. The reason, quite simply, is that a Perfect Storm has been brewing in geriatric care in recent years and will begin wreaking havoc just as the Boomers reach sixty-five.

The implications for you and your family are that you are going to need a real sense of urgency to plan and prepare for a whole new set of challenges when you enter your last chapter.

Here are the phenomena that power the Boomers' Perfect Storm:

1. Escalating demand for resource-intensive health care

Starting in 2010, the seventy-seven million members of the Baby Boom generation began their march into retirement. This unprecedented demographic movement will have a profound impact on American society and its health care system for generations to come.

- In 2011 alone, the number of people in the United States celebrating their sixty-fifth birthday jumped 21 percent, from 2.7 million to 3.3 million, according to the Census Bureau.

- The ranks of retirees are projected to double in the next three decades, from thirty-six million to seventy million, comprising 20 percent of the population, compared to 13 percent today.

- The eighty-five-and-older population will be our fastest-growing segment, projected to grow from four million to nineteen million in 2050, according to the National Center for Health Statistics.

The implications of this tidal wave of new geriatric patients are momentous, not only because of the sheer numbers, but also because the type of health care that the average retiree requires is many times more resource-intensive than for the average American:

- the 13 percent of our population over sixty-five today accounts for:

  o 44 percent of hospital care

  o 38 percent of emergency medical service responses

  o 35 percent of prescriptions

  o 26 percent of physician visits

Further, it's important to point out that there is a relatively high percentage of low-tech demands in geriatric care. Particularly when the parent reaches the assisted-living stage of life, with needs like bathing assistance, meal preparation, transportation, and social services, caregiving is still a one-on-one personal interaction process. While personal care is absolutely necessary to the health and well-being of the patient, it is not particularly responsive to technological breakthrough.

Finally, it's worth noting that in general, the number of family caregivers is dwindling.

- Americans are having smaller families than in generations past.

- Greater geographical mobility means your kids may be dispersed across the country and less available for caregiving.

- Dual-career households, while good for the pocketbook, mean that the traditional stay-at-home wife taking care of Mom and Dad is no longer an option.

While the ramifications of the Boomer takeover of the retirement segment may be multilayered, complicated, and daunting for the health care community, it is quite simple for you and your family as you enter your last chapter: From now on, the competition for geriatric health care resources will become ever fiercer with each passing year.

You and your kids need to start preparing.

2. Boomers' longer last chapter

The duration of the "elderly" years has mushroomed over the past three decades, as life expectancies have increased and older Americans have stayed healthier. In fact, an American who reaches age sixty-five can expect to live on average another 18.5 years (16.8 for men, 19.8 for women), according to the National Center for Health Statistics.

However, there is a downside to all those extra years. The fundamental cause behind this longevity is that, due to groundbreaking medical advancements in detection, diagnosis, and treatment, along with a more concerted commitment to healthy living, people are dying "gradually" rather than "suddenly," as was the norm in previous generations. For example, according to an annual study by the Centers for Disease Control and Prevention, death from heart attacks has dropped 61 percent from the rates of thirty years ago. Stroke fatalities declined even further (71 percent) over the same period.

Of course, people are still dying; they're just taking longer to do it. In recent years, "incremental killers" have become much more common:

- Chronic respiratory disease increased 77 percent in the last fifteen years

- Deaths from Alzheimer's doubled in the last twenty-five years, and are expected to triple by midcentury

- Cancer deaths increased 22 percent over the last thirty years

The upshot is that the cost implications of living longer lives are significant. As older Americans become a larger proportion of the population, the resulting increase in people with chronic health conditions like Parkinson's disease, arthritis, diabetes, heart disease, and almost all types of cancer will create a huge demand for health care and social services.

The implication for you and your family is that with increased years of retirement will very likely come a greater need for the family to cover assisted-living and medical expenses.

You and your kids need to start preparing.

3. Declining supply of medical practitioners

What ultimately whips the world of geriatric care into a perfect storm is that exploding demand is about to run into faltering supply.

Over the next thirty years, the Baby Boomers' sheer numbers and the extent and duration of their medical requirements will drive up the need for quality health care exponentially. Yet practitioners who deliver geriatric medical care—primary-care physicians, nurse practitioners, and geriatricians—are already in short supply and are projected to fall further behind exploding demand.

Projected growth in population vs. doctors

60% increase from 2010

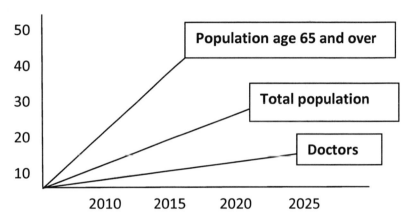

<u>Primary-care Physicians</u>

The primary care physician is critical to care management of chronic conditions that seniors will inevitably face. Yet, just as the Boomers are entering this phase of their lives, medical students have been opting for the specialties.

In 1960, half of all physicians in the country were in primary care. By 1978, the percentage had fallen to 36 percent, and in 2008 down to 32 percent.

The root causes for this migration appear to be a combination of lifestyle and compensation. Specialists have shorter hours and no on-call schedules. Yet their median income sits at $305,575, versus $194,409 for primary-care physicians, according to a 2010 survey by the Medical Group Management Association.

So it should be no surprise that today, according to a 2009 study by the Journal of the American Medical Association, only 2 percent of the graduating classes of medical schools are entering residency training in primary care.

But there's also a qualitative challenge that Boomers will need to confront, as described by an internist in one of my focus groups:

> *Because fees are fixed by Medicare and insurers, the only way primary-care doctors can generate more revenue is to take on more patients, which means spending less time with each one. Yet the most common complaint you hear from patients is, "I don't have enough time with the doctor."*

> *They're right. You can't take good care of your patients with chronic conditions in less than fifteen minutes.*

Nurses

The picture for Boomers is equally dire in the nursing profession. Today, 13 percent of nursing positions nationwide are vacant; 20 percent are likely to go unfilled by 2015, according to the American Hospital Association.

To make matters worse, dramatic technological improvements in health care in the last twenty years mean even more nurses are required, especially ones with comprehensive training, because there are more diagnostic tests to run, more medications to administer, and more machines to monitor.

Geriatric Specialists

Finally, there are the geriatricians, doctors who have taken an additional year of training after a three-year residency in family or internal medicine. In many ways, this practitioner group is uniquely qualified to treat seniors, since, rather than just focusing on cures, they also spend time managing patients' inevitable decline, helping them to maintain their independence and to age as well as possible.

Yet because geriatricians average $162,500 a year in salary, about half of what radiologists, gastroenterologists, and cardiologists make (according to the American Medical Group Association), their numbers have fallen by one-third in recent years. In fact, today there are only 7,600 geriatricians nationwide, not enough to meet current demand, and far below the 36,000 needed by 2030, according to the American Geriatrics Society.

The clear implications for you and your family are that the days of your doctor providing continuity of care and guiding you through the complex medical system are most likely numbered, leaving you to navigate on your own.

You and your kids need to start preparing.

You should have the Other Talk now; then keep on talking!

4. Available public resources for the Boomers' last chapter

Starting in 2010, an enormous segment (43 percent) of the working population began to retire and transform from taxpayers to government beneficiaries. Because each of the next two generations is 15 percent smaller, the workforce will grow more slowly, as will tax revenues to finance Medicare, Medicaid, and Social Security.

At the same time, health care inflation, which is driving up the bill for Medicare and Medicaid, will send the budget deficit skyrocketing.

While we won't know the outcome of the current debate about medical spending priorities and budget deficits raging in Congress and across the country, perhaps for years to come, it's obvious that changes to the delivery of medical care to senior citizens will occur.

One thing we do know for certain: The rules of the game and public resources available for the Boomers' last chapter will look vastly different than they do today.

You and your kids need to start preparing.

You should have the Other Talk now; then keep on talking!

<u>Conclusion</u>

The medical delivery system is approaching a tipping point, beyond which patients will face dangerously long wait times and distances to see physicians. Or they will get more care from nurses, physician assistants, and other substitutes, whose ranks are already stretched thin. Or they will go without.

The other devil in the details is that it doesn't matter how good your insurance coverage is if availability and access to quality health care are becoming increasingly limited.

You need a game changer if you are to successfully navigate the medical and many other challenges that you will face in your last chapter.

The Other Talk is one important tool to help you achieve that, because you need partners (your kids) and a plan that prepares you and your family for the roles you all will play in your last chapter.

And because you can't know how things will turn out, you'll need to have the Other Talk on an ongoing basis.

The next six chapters will show you how.

Getting Ready for the Other Talk

CHAPTER FIVE

SETTING THE STAGE FOR THE OTHER TALK

Current conventional wisdom has it that the Baby Boomer generation will age differently than their parents. We will have a more active lifestyle, more dollars to spend on it, and more years to enjoy it.

However, there is one aspect of aging in which we Boomers will surely follow in the footsteps of all previous generations. Like every elderly parent in the history of mankind, Boomers will undoubtedly intone with somber and heartfelt conviction, "I don't want to be a burden to my kids."

Well, get over it. You will be! Because as we cruise through our last chapter of life, we will need help—and plenty of it.

Margaret, a social worker I interviewed from the South Side of Chicago, gave me a sense of reality by laying out the breadth and depth of what's involved.

It's a full-time job when you are looking out for people with long-term care needs who are chronic and elderly and declining . . . from the handling of their day-to-day care, to running the gauntlet of insurance, Medicare and Medicaid forms and regulations, to learning about various diseases and the myriad of alternative (and often conflicting) treatments to the managing of medications and doctor visits.

It's a full-time job! And all this at a time when the adult child is scrambling to keep the many balls in his or her own life (like kids, spouse, household, career) from crashing to the ground.

Of course, the way to reduce the weight of this burdensome responsibility is to start *now* to have the Other Talk. By brainstorming and fleshing out the contingencies, preparing for the surprises, and making your last chapter of life a time for your family to enjoy together, not just a trauma to stumble through, you will be lightening the load considerably.

Yet there seems to be a catch-22 in play whenever this conversation is contemplated.

On the one hand, I have found the basic concept and construct of the Other Talk meets with nearly universal enthusiasm, whether I'm talking with colleagues in the elder care, hospice, and funeral service industries, with professionals in the publishing and academic worlds, with typical Baby Boomers, or even with their Gen X kids. They get it:

- The wisdom of involving your kids in the issues and decisions that come up during your last chapter

- The tremendous emotional benefits of avoiding family feuds, financial surprises, and philosophical disagreements

- The ability to focus on the living to be done rather than the dying to be feared

However, on the other hand, I also know from my research with families that the theory of the Other Talk rarely translates into practice.

It's as if a locked door stands between the parents and the kids. One or maybe both parties may actually want to engage in the conversation. But what causes them to hold back are the very difficult emotional issues and various fears of the unknown that can bubble up around the end of life.

That's why it's critical that you do a good deal of emotional and strategic preparation before you are ready to open the door to the Other Talk.

There are four steps to effectively setting this stage:

1. Start with your own mental state

2. Factor in the kids' emotions

3. Establish a frame of reference

4. Adopt a comfortable tone

1. Start with your own mental state

Just as your kids did when you sat them down for that first "birds and the bees" talk, they will take cues and clues on how open and comfortable you are in discussing your last chapter and, therefore, how willing they are to participate in it.

As a result, before you can initiate the Other Talk, you'll need to confront and ultimately come to grips with two practical yet emotion-laden issues.

<u>Role Reversal</u>

Many of us define ourselves by our accomplishments, our skill at getting things done, and our ability to develop creative solutions to complex problems. These barometers of success translate into power and control over our lives, and ultimately our sense of self-worth.

Therefore, when we agree to the reversal of roles with our kids, however willingly, there is a tendency to feel that turning over power and control for decision making will result in a downsizing of our self-image.

As a consequence, even for the parent who acknowledges the need and inevitability of role reversal, it can still carry the stigma of, "I am no longer who I was!"

A good example of this internal conflict is Dan, a successful entrepreneur in Seattle, who recently signed over financial and medical powers of attorney to his eldest son. In addition, Dan, along with his wife, Shari, moved out of their three-story house into a well-appointed assisted-living facility. He had done all of this voluntarily after several conversations with his doctor, financial advisers, and extended family, but clearly felt a deep sense of loss.

I know Shari and I need assistance at this point in our lives, but, damn it, I feel like I had to give up a huge part of me.

I've always been proud of my accomplishments, growing the company from two to two hundred people, attracting great young talent, positioning it as a player on the national stage. And I really enjoyed my success in the stock market.

Now my affairs are managed by my kids—and I deeply appreciate the time and energy that they put into it. But there are times when I want to stand up and scream, "You can't tell me what to do. I changed your diapers!"

Clearly, the notion of role reversal can stir up some serious emotional reactions.

That's why the Other Talk puts it front and center in the conversation. The intended consequence is that when the time comes to shift decision-making responsibilities, it is accomplished more like the smooth transition of a pendulum, rather than an abrupt hitting-the-wall at the "moment of crisis." To ensure a comfortable pendulum swing, you should reconcile yourself to role reversal on three levels.

First, openly acknowledge the inevitability of ceding the decision making and management of the day-today responsibilities to your kids. This will act to focus you on planning to hand off, rather than grappling to hang on.

Second, establish ground rules on the potential circumstances or trigger points that will affect the change of responsibilities in key functions, such as bill paying, transportation, living arrangements, money and asset management, and medical decisions.

Finally, embrace your plan for role reversal as liberating, not denigrating. It's not the loss of power and control; it's the gain of security and freedom. It's not about where the pendulum is swinging from; it's where the pendulum is headed.

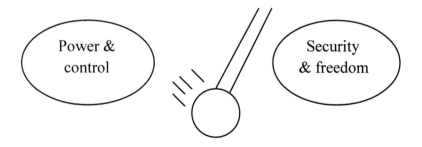

Full financial disclosure

The other hurdle that you need to get over is when and how much of your financial situation you are willing to share with your kids. (The irony, of course, is that your financial reality, good or bad, will end up on your kids' plate anyway.) The short answer if you are serious about having the Other Talk is, "Now, and everything."

This is apparently easier said than done. When I asked my research respondents whether they had shared their financial reality with their kids, they came up with a variety of excuses for why they hadn't.

- "It's none of their business." (My response: "It will be.")

- "I'm embarrassed that I didn't save enough for retirement." (My response: "That's a really excellent reason why they *should* know!")

- "My kids aren't capable of managing financial details." (My response: "Your family definitely needs a plan, and maybe some outside help.")

- "Telling my kids how large the estate is could have unintended consequences on their lifestyle and motivations." (My response: "Discussing family finances now will be much better than waiting until after the sibling battle lines form.")

To a large extent, the Other Talk is about contingency planning. Without having a thorough discussion with your kids now about your financial situation, you're essentially tying one hand behind their backs just as they are getting ready to take on more responsibilities in your last chapter.

You need to prepare yourself to work with your kids *now* to understand what's available financially, introduce them to any financial advisers you might have, and educate them on your asset allocation and spending strategies. That's the partnership that the Other Talk is designed to achieve between you and your kids.

2. Factoring in the kids' emotions

Once you've gotten your own head straight with the emotional hurdles of role reversal and financial disclosure, it's time to consider the kids' mind-set on the eve of the Other Talk. As you get ready to unlock that door, swing it open, and invite the kids in for your first "last chapter" conversation, it's important that you think about how to prepare them mentally and emotionally for the subject matter.

To begin with, you need to recognize that every question or issue related to the end of your life, however mundane, is a mix of practical and emotional. In fact, you can expect a jumble of reactions that can be wide-ranging and, at times, contradictory:

> Fear
> Sadness
> Nervousness
> Anger
> Queasiness
> Panic
> Revulsion

Why this bewildering array of seemingly disparate reactions? Because you're talking about coping with a period of undetermined time that may include several stages, but with an endgame where your kids are left without a parent.

There's also another emotional dimension to the Other Talk. Kids can become overwhelmed with feelings of responsibility, guilt, inadequacy, embarrassment, and resentment as the fear and foreboding of what is to come next pulls into view.

For both emotional traumas, loss of a parent and the burden of caregiving, it's critical that you carefully prepare your kids for the Other Talk. You'll need to think about which issues are troubling or even terrifying, and to which child. You'll need to help the family get past the fear of confronting your mortality; of brushing up against the issues of power, control, and financial limitations; of visualizing what it will be like when you are gone.

My first suggestion to get your kids ready emotionally is only slightly self-serving, since it has been reported to be very effective by a number of families who have reviewed this book: Give your kids a copy of this book to read *before* you sit down for the Other Talk.

This technique seems to help pave the way because your kids are able to explore and embrace the philosophy of proactively dealing with your last chapter before it happens. It allows them to deal with the hypothetical before confronting their eventual reality.

My second suggestion is that you discuss with your spouse how your individual attitudes, desires, and opinions may differ, sometimes markedly, and how they should be woven into the conversation in a way that doesn't cause confusion or conflict. What you don't want to do is confront all these issues for the first time in front of the kids.

My third suggestion is to encourage your kids to adapt the

collaborative theme inherent in the Other Talk in terms of how they might work with their brothers and sisters in your last chapter. We know definitively that the impact of being saddled, often unexpectedly, with the parent care burden can have serious repercussions among siblings.

According to a recent National Alliance for Caregiving and AARP study, 17 percent of adult children said the responsibility of caring for their parent had taken a toll on their health, while 31 percent described the situation as emotionally stressful. Two-thirds of those solo caregivers who had jobs said they had gone to work late, left early, or taken time off because of their caregiving responsibilities. Finally, 10 percent of all parental caregivers say there is not an equal division of labor (translation: sibling resentment).

It doesn't have to be this way. Recently I witnessed how the Other Talk can help create a sense of purpose and cooperation with a family I spoke with in Phoenix. The son, Robert, assumed responsibility for his mother's finances. Sister Vanessa handled the medical appointments. The youngest, Christy, acted as the day-to-day contact for the home-health-care nurses. This setup not only achieved collaboration of effort and commitment; it also avoided overwhelming one primary caregiver, typically a daughter, or the child who lives closest to the parents.

3. Establishing a frame of reference

The next step in your preparation is to frame the conversation and the participants' role in it so that you can:

- Achieve better outcomes and less panic and stress

- Manage your affairs the way you intend, and avoid choices you don't want

- Ensure that everyone contributes in ways that match their interests, skill set, and comfort zone

Additionally, it's important to establish that the Other Talk is not a onetime event, à la the birds-and-the-bees drive-by, with books on the bed and, "Any questions?" Rather, it is an ongoing, dynamic dialogue, because:

o Your physical and financial condition will likely change in unexpected ways

o Your assumptions and beliefs may evolve over time

o The availability of your kids may change due to shifting job and family responsibilities, resources, and geographic location

Finally, because you want to be proactive in managing the last chapter, not just reactive to tomorrow's surprises or emergencies, you and your kids should plan to commit time and energy to two fundamental functions.

<u>Knowledge Base</u>

As I mentioned in chapter four, "Navigating the Boomers' Perfect Storm," the dynamics of geriatric care are going to change dramatically in the years ahead as a result of:

1. Escalating demand for resource-intensive health care

2. Longer-living elderly/chronic-care patients

3. Declining supply of geriatric practitioners

4. Questionable availability of public resources for the elderly

As a result, the rules of the game are changing, and to a large extent, you and your family will be on your own to figure out options and answers. There will be so much to learn and organize and be current on. That's why staying on top of your options, emerging medical treatments, and changing legal and financial regulations will become a critical ongoing function for the entire family.

In fact, I would suggest that the Other Talk is the place to start parceling out research assignments, and, in subsequent Other Talks, where you all can come together to review, update, and cross-reference your knowledge base.

To give you a sense of how extensive this imperative will most likely be for you, let me introduce Carly, a forty-five-year-old accountant and daughter of a Parkinson's patient.

> *I have a binder that's about four inches thick, with all the things that I had to find out about in all these different areas, from insurance forms, rules, and regulations, to new medical treatments, new sources of funding, new living arrangements, to speech therapists, occupational therapists, physical therapists, to Medicare, Dad's pension, Social Security.*
>
> *It's relentless, it's overwhelming . . . and absolutely essential.*

Trigger Points

Perhaps one of the most challenging issues that your family will face in your last chapter is how and when to shift decision making from you to your kids. That's why a key dimension of the Other Talk is to establish criteria that will trigger the decisions to reassign roles and responsibilities.

The intended result is to avoid your feeling threatened and confrontational when the time comes to make a change, because you've already agreed to it up front.

To begin with, it is important to recognize that role reversal doesn't need to be a onetime wholesale changing of the guard, but can be a series of trigger points for the various functions of day-to-day living (i.e., paying the bills, turning to assisted living, moving out of your house, etc.).

The essence of trigger points is that you and your kids thoroughly discuss and jointly decide how and when a particular responsibility is to be shifted. In this way, your entire family feels part of the decision and can take ownership in its implementation.

While I'll be discussing the trigger-point concept in later chapters, let me demonstrate how it can work with what is often the opening act in a family's role reversal: giving up the car keys.

For your kids, the decision for you to stop driving has important practical implications. It means that your loss of mobility will require your children to come up with alternate forms of transportation, either chauffeuring, if they live in town or depending on friends, neighbors, and public transport if they're not.

For you, this change of life is more cerebral, more fundamental. Here's my personal take on it.

> I love driving, especially in my blue sports car, a Nissan 350Z.
>
> I love the freedom of getting up and going whenever I want.
>
> I love the sensation of smoothly shifting through six

gears.

I love the power of the acceleration.

I love the control in taking whatever route I want.

I love the sense of pride in keeping my car in mint condition.

So when I contemplate the possibility that a time will come when I shouldn't be driving, when my eyesight, motor skills and reaction time reach the point that I'm endangering myself and others inside and outside the car, I get despondent and depressed, then angry at the prospect of having one of life's great pleasures taken away from me.

But then I remember the near-calamities that my parents experienced

1. While wintering in Arizona, Mom came home from shopping one day with the entire right side of the car ripped up. She had no idea how it happened, or that it even occurred. It turned out her rapidly escalating and undiagnosed Alzheimer's played a central role.

2. Early one summer morning in Michigan, Dad, whose MS was causing vivid hallucinations, sneaked out at four a.m. to take a spin to his favorite park. Once there, he couldn't remember how to get home, so he (fortunately) waited for us to come find him. It all made for a frantic four hours for the rest of the family.

Rather than put myself and my family in those situations, I've decided to establish criteria with my wife and daughter that will help me transition out of the driver's seat. We've even put it in writing to avoid any misunderstanding on their part or backsliding on mine.

1. Annual eye exam that meets driver's license requirements

2. Test for motor skills and mental acuity as part of my annual physical

Will I miss zipping around in my sports car when the time comes to be a full-time passenger? You bet.

But I also know that laying down this trigger point now and sharing it with my family will be far easier than scaring them into a "taking away the car keys" confrontation because of some crazy or even lethal driving stunt that I inadvertently performed.

4. Adopting a comfortable tone

Now that you have thought through the emotional barriers for each of the participants, as well as a structure that will bring the family together, you are ready to develop the atmospherics.

Of course, each family will approach the Other Talk in its own way and on its own terms. But I have found that the most productive and comfortable conversations occurred because the parents spent time creating a welcoming and involving environment for their kids.

There are a number of dimensions that you will want to weave together:

Informal	To reduce potential angst and meeting paralysis in your children, it's important that you position the Other Talk as a relaxed, thoughtful, wide-ranging dialogue on a variety of issues that lie ahead.
Informative	Family members can engage in an open, honest discussion that clears away potential misunderstandings and wrong assumptions that often result in festering resentments and financial missteps down the road.
Collaborative	The Other Talk is about the rest of your life, not just the end of it. As a result, you have the unique opportunity to explore how you want to live your last chapter, and what experiences you want to share with your kids as it unfolds.
Productive	The more you and your kids anticipate potential twists and turns *before* infirmities set in, the more likely all of you will navigate that last chapter with skill, creativity, and confidence.
Loving	The Other Talk should strike a balance between taking care of business and

~~performing an act of love and affection for~~
your kids.

Empowering   While the Other Talk is about you, it also offers a number of life lessons that could benefit your kids in their own lives:

1. It teaches them to be flexible and adaptable as things change in unexpected ways

2. It enables them to make the tough decisions, if and when you can't

3. It establishes a template from which they can discuss, explore, educate, and think about end-of-life issues with their own children

4. It demonstrates that "taking care of the kids after I'm gone" isn't just a financial issue

5. It adds a dimension to your family relationship that most kids will never know

In essence, the Other Talk is designed to break the typical elder-care pattern of lurching from one crisis to the next. It gives your kids the self-confidence, the knowledge, the tools, and the perspective to take on the responsibility when the role-reversal process begins to take place.

More important, by preparing for the decisions, the possibilities, and the responsibilities in the last chapter of your life, both you and your kids can focus on the living to be done, the accomplishments that have yet to be achieved, and the memory and the legacy that will make the family proud.

CHAPTER SIX

GETTING YOUR DOCUMENTS IN ORDER

As you will discover when you sit down with your kids to have the Other Talk, there will be a number of "plumbing issues" that will come up. As a result, you will want to prepare yourself to intelligently address and be able to discuss them at some length—questions like:

- Do your will, living will, and powers of attorney (financial and medical) exist, and are they up-to-date?

- What key elements and strategies of your financial plan are designed to ensure that you don't outlive your money?

- Is your inventory of documents, family advisers and phone numbers, safety box locations, and insurance readily available?

– Have you made any prearrangements for a funeral service, including personal preferences, instructions, and payments?

The bottom line is that you should plan to spend some time *before* the Other Talk collating and organizing a variety of documents that will give your kids a snapshot of your current situation. Further, it will provide them ready access to legal documents if you become incapacitated or when you reach that last sentence.

Sense of Urgency versus Completeness of Documentation

I have one caveat before you start accumulating documents.

It will become clear from reviewing the following pages that finding or requesting or generating the proper, up-to-date documentation will most likely be a time-consuming and, at times, frustrating process. What I *don't* want you to do is to put off the Other Talk until you get every last scrap of paper organized, duplicated, and bound into a notebook for each child.

Those notebooks (either paper or electronic,) of course, need to be produced, because until you put everything together, you have not fully armed your kids to take on the various responsibilities as your last chapter unfolds. But the notebook is not the goal; it is merely a means to an end.

As you begin the accumulation process, I want you to stay focused on one singular objective:

The more information your kids have, and *the sooner they get it, the better for you and for them.*

That's why you need to commit yourself and your family, right here, right now, to having the Other Talk within the next three months with as much documentation as you can pull together.

Waiting until the binders are complete is just another form of procrastination, one with potentially serious consequences. Here's how Darlene, a senior marketing executive, described the price she and her sisters ended up paying:

> *By the time we found out how sick Mom was, she went into a coma. We had no idea if she had a will, a living will, powers of attorney, or, if she did, where to find them. We had no clue about her financial dealings or situation. So we were flying blind, having to make all the decisions for her.*
>
> *When you've got all this illness thrust on you all at once, the pressure to make the right calls (the ones Mom would have wanted but never told us) and the need to take on the day-to-day responsibilities become truly overwhelming.*

What Could Go into the Notebooks?

With that in mind, it's time to get to work. The list of documents described in the next few pages is not intended to be definitive or represent expert advice. You should talk with any financial, legal, and accounting advisers you may have about how to meet your individual needs.

However, this list *is* designed to get you started thinking about the wealth of information you need to prepare and bring to the Other Talk. Further, you will want to review and update these documents annually for the subsequent Other Talks in order to reflect changes in your assets and in your preferences.

The Will

An original will is the most important document you need to keep on file. You need to let your kids know where it is located and, I would strongly recommend, share it with them now to avoid misunderstandings, resentments, and legal actions after you're gone.

This document allows you to dictate who inherits your assets. Dying without a will means that state law and the legal system will decide what happens. Further, not having the original document means that family members can challenge a copy of a will in court.

Medical

1. Advance directives

   There are two key documents that you will want to fill out and give to your kids at the Other Talk:

a. durable health care power of attorney, which allows your designee to make health care decisions on your behalf if you are incapacitated

b. a living will, which details your wishes at the end of life, often including a "do not resuscitate" (DNR) order

In addition to your family, you should also give these advance directives to your primary-care doctor so it can be included in your medical record.

Further, if you have scheduled surgery or other planned hospital admissions, you should bring copies with you, to make it part of your medical chart.

2. Doctors

You will want to create a summary of each of your doctors and other medical advisers that includes:

– name and contact information

– medical specialty

– brief description of your diagnosis

– treatment plan and time line

3. Medications

You need to develop a prescription summary that

includes:

- type and strength of medication

- what the medication is treating

- location of prescription refills (pharmacy or mail order)

- physician who wrote the prescription

Financial

You need to provide contact information for key advisors (attorney, financial planner, accountant, stockbroker, real estate agent, etc.). Your kids will need the name, address, phone and fax numbers, and e-mail address for each of these individuals.

Key Documents

Your family needs to know where to find a variety of documents (the originals, and copies if applicable), since your kids won't be able to make decisions or take actions on your behalf without them

- Birth certificate

- Social Security card

- Marriage license

- If applicable, divorce judgment and decree, or the stipulation agreement if settled out of court

- Passport

- Trust documents

Insurance for life, health, home, vehicles, and boats

Family members will want to know the name of the carrier, the policy number, policy type and specifics, and the agent connected with each policy. Be sure to include any life or health policies granted by a company when you retired.

The availability of this information is critical, especially for life insurance, since insurers are not required to determine whether a policyholder has died. As a result, a claim is paid only when the surviving family members contact the company.

This nonpayment of claims is a bigger problem than you might think. More than $400 million in unclaimed life insurance payments have piled up since 2000 in New York State alone.

Tax Returns

The kids will need to know the location of your most recent seven years of returns. This is necessary for IRS queries, but also helpful, when the time comes, to determine the extent of assets in the estate and in filing a final income tax and estate return and, if applicable, a revocable-trust return.

Banking

Your family needs the location, account numbers, and contact information for each of your checking and savings accounts, as well as the location and contents of your safety-deposit box. Be sure to register your spouse's and kids' names with the bank, and get them to sign the registration document so they can gain access without a court order.

Proof of Ownership

You need to accumulate in a central location the original documentation of:

- housing and land ownership deeds

- cemetery plots

- vehicle and boat titles

- savings bonds

- partnership or corporate operating agreements

Investment, Pension and Loan Information

Your heirs will need to know the location of:

- an inventory of current investments, including taxable and traditional and Roth IRA accounts, 401(k) and 403(b), plus the account numbers and the contact information for who handles each

- your latest statement from Social Security

- company pension plan details and contact information

- original mortgage and any home equity loans and most recent refinancing details

- a summary of loans you have outstanding and the repayment terms

- a summary of debts you owe (wills and living trusts should be written to direct how debts are to be settled)

Credit Card Information

You should make front-and-back copies of all active credit cards and indicate the location of the most recent statement, especially if there is an outstanding balance.

Valuable Items

You will want to provide your family with a summary of antiques, jewelry, original artwork, family heirlooms, etc., along with the most current appraisals.

Burial and Funeral Information

Certainly your kids will want to honor your wishes at the end of life. That's why you need to summarize choices on:

- cremation or burial

- type of service (where, what kind, visitation, specific music and/or readings, military proceedings, etc.)

- organ donation arrangements and time frame

- location of burial plot, type of grave marker

- charity donation in lieu of flowers

In addition, you will want to let your kids know if you have prepaid for a funeral service or taken out burial insurance, and with whom. Just like the life insurance companies, these prepaid providers are under no obligation to contact the family, and will pocket the proceeds if no request is made. (This actually happened to my family, even though both parents had paid in full.)

To conclude, I want to encourage you to schedule the Other Talk within the next three months with as much documentation as you can pull together.

However, since there will undoubtedly be information gaps that will need to be filled in, I'd ask you to add to your preliminary notebook a page that lays out a timetable for its completion. Only then have you fully armed your kids to take on the various responsibilities as your last chapter unfolds.

The more information your kids have and *the* sooner *they get it, the better for you and for them.*

Turning the Other Talk into an Action Plan

CHAPTER SEVEN

FINANCING YOUR UNCERTAIN FUTURE

One of the most complex and daunting challenges that we face as we get older is trying to figure out how to manage our money in our last chapter of life. The problem, quite simply, is that the end zone (when, where, and how) as well as the associated costs are unknowable.

Sadly, many people deal with this financial conundrum the same way they approach other challenges in the last chapter of life: with healthy doses of procrastination and inertia.

In fact, it is estimated that 50 percent of Americans forty-five and older haven't even *tried* to calculate how much they will need to save in order to live comfortably in retirement, according to a March 2011 study by the Employee Benefit Research Institute.

Yet despite inaction by so many, it's a problem that is top of mind for most Americans. More than 81 percent of respondents to a recent *Consumer Reports* survey say they worry about being able to afford health care in retirement, and 68 percent worry that they'll go bankrupt paying for medical bills following a serious illness or accident.

Even the wealthier seem frozen in the headlights. Two-thirds of families with at least $250,000 in investable assets expressed concern that they would outlive their retirement nest egg, according to a June 2011 study by Bank of America Merrill Lynch.

Unfortunately, this fear of running out of money in your last chapter is not misplaced.

One out of every three bankruptcies in America is caused by overwhelming medical expenses.

I don't know about you, but I was stunned by this statistic. But then, as I began looking into the likely causes of this financial catastrophe, I realized that the Other Talk could not only play a significant role in overcoming the inertia over retirement planning, but also could directly address the worry of outlasting your assets.

Here's what I learned about the leading drivers of bankruptcy at the end of life:

1. The first cause is what the medical profession calls the "compression of morbidity." The layman's translation of this rather gruesome terminology is that the bulk of an individual's spending on health care will occur in that person's last two years, and especially the last six months.

   In other words, morbidity—the incidence of various illnesses—accelerates at the end of life, with multiple medical specialists getting into the act. This can become very costly, and is the reason that Medicare now spends nearly 27 percent of *its total budget* on patients in their last twelve months of life.

2. The second cause of financial problems at the end of life is that Americans approach their last chapter with a set of expectations that doesn't come close to reflecting reality, according to a recent TIAA-CREF study.

Retirement expectations

	Perception	Reality
My spending in retirement will:		
Decrease	56%	31%
Stay the same	36	47
Increase	8	22

What this analysis shows is that 56% of people in the study believed that their spending would decrease in retirement. The reality was that spending decreased for only 31% of respondents.

At the other end, only 8% of people in the study expected their spending to increase in their retirement. In reality, 22% of respondents saw their spending increase during this time.

The implication is that you will likely spend a lot

more in your last chapter than your financial assumptions allow for.

3. Finally, the elderly parent can get in trouble because he or she loses the mental capacity to control his or her finances.

   Ralph, one of my focus group participants, remembered standing by helplessly, watching his eighty-two-year-old mother drive her financial wagon off a cliff:

   > *She kept living like there was no tomorrow. She kept spending and spending and spending like she had it, except she didn't. Piling up debt on credit cards, buying cars she didn't need, continually overdrawing her bank account.*
   >
   > *It was a nightmare, but I didn't know how to stop her.*

How can you explicitly deal with these causes of financial ruin?

- Ralph's innocent bystander/inertia

- the tendency toward unrealistic spending expectations

- the potential health care train wreck in the last year or so of life.

Essentially, you need a plan—not a static one, but rather a dynamic one that includes your spouse and your kids, who will be instrumental in implementing it.

What you don't need is a "number," an idea that was made fleetingly popular in 2006 by a book of the same name. In *The Number: A Completely Different Way to Think about the Rest of Your Life*, author Lee Eisenberg purported to divine a way to "determine how much money you need to secure the rest of your life." In my view, coming up with a singular "number" is a good start, but considering it the answer to retirement planning is naive and potentially dangerous. Just ask the families who went bankrupt in the last years of their parents' lives because of unplanned medical expenses.

What you need is the dynamism of the Other Talk, which is about *managing evolution* in your last chapter of life:

- decision making
- roles and responsibilities
- asset management
- living arrangements
- health care needs

What you need is the adaptability and flexibility inherent in the Other Talk process, which you can achieve by committing to annual updates. This will ensure that you and your family can revisit your assumptions and financial condition so that you can recalibrate your plan if the current reality requires it.

Finally, what you need to remember is that the Other Talk isn't just about the orderly distribution of your assets while you're alive and when you are gone. It's also a means to an end:

- how to get the most out of the rest of your life

- how to involve your kids in that adventure

The "Financing Your Uncertain Future" Discussion

Fundamentally, this part of the Other Talk should be focused on a series of "what if" scenarios, because your situation in your last chapter is forever fluid.

- Physically your condition will evolve, requiring various levels and types of medical care.

- Social Security and Medicare benefits may change; tax rates and policies may be rewritten.

- Real estate valuations can reverse course (remember when conventional wisdom held that housing prices would never go down?).

- The investment environment can be unpredictably volatile (conventional wisdom had it that stocks in the long term would return a reliable 7 percent return, yet in the last ten years the Dow Jones Industrial Average has barely moved).

Spending Priorities

As a result, in preparing for the "financing your uncertain future" discussion, I recommend that you bring a contingency planning mind-set as you ponder the guiding principle of this conversation:

What is the life you want, what is the life you don't want, and what are the costs of each?

To answer this question, you need to establish a clear picture of your financial situation, develop a series of "what if" scenarios of what you want to accomplish and experience, then determine how realistically these various scenarios can exist within your financial reality.

For example, the life you want may be three overseas trips every year, plus a house in the country. The life you don't want may be living in a nursing home and giving up driving your car. However, when you run the numbers, you realize that the costs of international travel, a second home, eventual twenty-four/seven care in your home, and keeping a car will consume your assets by age seventy-one. You need to revisit the life you want and the one you don't.

Or perhaps you approached the aspirations of your last chapter more qualitatively:

I want my life to be busy, useful, flexible, relevant, always learning, physically active.

Of course, there are a number of ways to achieve those goals, each at different price points. Your job then is to pick and choose those that meet your budget.

However you think about the life you want, either quantitatively or qualitatively, I would recommend one more level of contingency planning. To maximize the fun and satisfaction in your last chapter, consider setting goals and priorities by decade. For example,

- adventure travel, like climbing the Inca Trail to Machu Picchu, in your sixties

- guided tours, like bike trips in the Michigan countryside, in your seventies

- theater and museum trips in your eighties

- extreme bingo in your nineties

Certainly, your health and wealth will dictate whether your timetable speeds up or slows down, but at least you won't be waiting to strike out on some adventure until it's too late for you physically or financially.

Perhaps the most important thing to keep in mind as you consider your dreams, goals, and aspirations is that the path to true happiness can be found in a lyric from a Sheryl Crow song:

> *It's not having what you want;*
> *it's wanting what you've got.*

Retirement Income Plan

Whichever tack you take to your spending priorities, you're not finished yet. You need to bring that same "what if" mind-set to your assets, to your budget, because the world is not a static place and neither is your pile of money.

You need to analyze your nest egg to determine whether you will outlive it or vice versa. To achieve that, there are a number of variables to consider that, not too many years ago, made this exercise a daunting and imprecise task.

Fortunately, in this age of computer modeling, creating "what if" scenarios has become fairly easy and straightforward. There are now software programs, often offered free of charge by brokerages, insurance companies, and financial planners, that can help you generate a series of nest-egg projections, depending on various spending assumptions and investment strategies.

Of course, you are going to need to do your homework, since your "what if" projections are only as good as the accuracy of the data you provide. Depending on the software you are using, the type of information you'll need to accumulate could include:

Annual expenses

- essential expenses
- discretionary expenses (e.g., travel, entertainment, clothes, etc.)
- supplemental health care insurance
- long-term health care insurance

Income

- Social Security benefits for husband and for wife (requires that you select a start date for taking the Social Security benefit, since it affects the size of payments for the rest of your life)

- pension benefits
- annuity income
- other income (e.g., dividends, interest, rental income, real estate sale including your home, etc.)

Current assets

- investment portfolio, including the dollar amount and percentage of total for stocks, bonds, and short-term instruments
- real estate
- other assets (e.g., antiques, artwork, etc.)
- level of risk you are comfortable with

Depending on the software program, you may be able to project the future value of your assets against various market-performance assumptions. More important, you may be able to estimate when your assets will be fully depleted.

Armed with these data, you can start working "what if" scenarios. For example:

- What happens if I change my retirement date?
- What happens if I change our annual spending rate?
- What happens if I change our asset mix?
- What happens if we convert from owning to renting?

Finally, these software programs are useful not only in estimating an end date for your nest egg, but also in encouraging you to revisit key decisions in your own personal retirement plan, including:

1. How long will you and your spouse live? According to an analysis by the Society of Actuaries, there is a 25 percent chance that a sixty-five-year-old in good health will live to:

   - ninety-two if male
   - ninety-four if female
   - ninety-seven if a surviving spouse from a married couple

2. Can your investment portfolio at least match the rate of inflation?

3. Have you established a withdrawal rate that won't jeopardize your long-term future?

4. Have you set aside funds to supplement Medicare and cover out-of-pocket health care costs, which Fidelity Investments estimate at $360,000 for a couple aged sixty-five who lives into their nineties?

5. Do you want to leave an inheritance for your kids, or is your goal like Rene's, one of my research respondents: "I want the last check that I write before I die to bounce!"

Planning for Role Reversal

Now that you've run due diligence on your financial plan, both spending priorities and the ability of your nest egg to deliver on them for *all* the years in your last chapter, it's time for you and your spouse to take one more step before you're ready to sit down with the family to have the Other Talk.

The two of you need to put a mechanism in place that shifts financial responsibilities from you to your kids with as little drama as possible, when the time comes. By building that mechanism *with* your children now, it will look like and feel like (and in fact be) prudent planning, rather than a fight over financial control.

If you postpone action, thinking. "I'll know when it's time," you will most likely find yourself out of the loop, losing your ability to guide an effective transition, because either:

- a sudden disability happened so fast that the rules of the game changed before you could react, or

- creeping dementia sneaked up on you

About half of Americans in their eighties have some form of dementia or cognitive decline. But problems usually start well before that. In a 2010 analysis that appeared in *The Wall Street Journal*, it was noted:

> *Recent research into our financial decision-making skills suggests they begin to slip after age 70 and suffer more rapid declines after 75, much as aging athletes lose speed and agility.*

As a result, your mental decline will be incremental, most

likely so gradual that you won't even notice (although those around you increasingly will). So, like the over-the-hill athlete who refuses to leave the game, you'll insist on maintaining your position until your kids are forced to drag you off the field.

Nobody wins that one. So let's consider the Other Talk approach.

Step One: Establishing a Financial Power of Attorney

If you have more than one child and all or some of them will be participating in the Other Talk, I recommend dividing up the responsibilities among them.

- One child could oversee the finances and handle all the bill paying.

- Another could monitor the medical diagnoses and treatments and stay on top of doctor visits.

- A third could be in charge of the home maintenance or be the liaison with the assisted-living-center arrangements.

That way all the kids have a responsibility, so nobody feels overburdened and eventually underappreciated, and the opportunities for sibling disagreements are reduced.

When choosing the child who will handle your finances (I'll get to the other two choices in later chapters), Linda Kaare, a Michigan elder-care attorney, urges that you should select "someone who is organized, dependable, and trustworthy, and is financially stable in his or her own life."

In addition, you should be honest about the amount of work and the challenges involved. When it came time for me to take over the financial responsibilities for my parents, I found the task fairly time-consuming and ongoing, with paying the bills, making investment decisions, and filing tax returns, especially since my parents and I lived in different states.

However, there are shortcuts, like electronic banking, that:

- execute automatic withdrawals for recurring expenses, like home health care, utilities, and phone bills

- allow you to monitor your parents' accounts for correct deposits and withdrawals

In addition, keeping an eye on the money can help you protect your parents from financial scams that target seniors, which have become so prevalent that the National Council on Aging (NCOA) calls it

The Crime of the 21st Century! Why? Because seniors are thought to have a significant amount of money sitting in their accounts. Financial scams also often go unreported or can be difficult to prosecute, so they're considered a low risk crime.

However, they are devastating to many older adults and can leave them in a very vulnerable and

unrecoverable position, since if you lose your money in your older years, there are very few options for earning new funds to replace what was lost.

Here's just one example from NCOA's top-ten list of how easy it is for someone in the last chapter of life to be separated from his or her money:

> **The Grandparent Scam** is so simple and so underhanded, because it uses one of older adults' most reliable assets, their hearts. Scammers will place a call to an older person and when the mark picks up, they will say something along the lines of: "Hi, Grandma, do you know who this is?" When the unsuspecting grandparent guesses the name of the grandchild the scammer most sounds like, the scammer has established a fake identity without having done a lick of background research.
>
> Once "in," the fake grandchild will usually ask for money to solve some unexpected financial problem (overdue rent, payment for car repairs, etc.), to be paid via Western Union or MoneyGram, which don't always require identification to collect. At the same time, the scam artist will beg the grandparent, "Please don't tell my parents; they would kill me."

Once you have settled on which of your children you want to help you manage the finances, *and* that child has agreed to take on that responsibility, you need to make your choice known to the family. Then you should move on three fronts, and I urge you to act quickly. It seems that assigning a financial power of attorney is an easy task to procrastinate. According to AARP, 73 percent of Americans forty-five years and older haven't gotten around to it.

1. Documentation

   To begin with, you should execute a financial power of attorney, which is basically a written, signed, and notarized document through which the parents give the designated child the authority to manage the parents' money: the right to do everything from writing checks to selling securities. Power of attorney can be effective immediately, or upon incapacity.

   Because you can write your own definition of "incapacity," I would strongly encourage you to get this document as soon as possible. The most common definition requires two physicians to declare the person incapacitated.

   Power of attorney documents are usually drafted by lawyers, but they don't have to be. You can find templates on the Internet, as outlined in the appendix.

2. Financial assistance

   The second front you should move on in the near term is to sit all your kids down for face-to-face meetings with your financial advisers: banker, lawyer, broker, accountant, insurance agent, financial planner, etc. The purpose is to get acquainted in preparation for future dealings, and to understand your financial strategies, tactics, and how things work.

If you don't currently use advisers, you should at least discuss the pros and cons of getting financial assistance when you first get together for the Other Talk. You may decide that outsourcing some of your financial decision making and execution may not only provide you and your kids with useful expertise, but also reduce familial friction and leave time for all of you to do other things.

3. Asset distribution

The third point to make with your kids, especially the one handling the finances, is that under current U.S. law, spouses who are American citizens can pass unlimited assets to each other, either during their lifetime or after death. However, distributing assets to other beneficiaries, including the children, is subject to certain limitations. To understand the rules, you and the kids should consult with a tax and/or financial planning expert.

Step Two: Simplifying Your Finances

As you probably discovered when you began to put together the notebooks that I discussed in chapter six, "Getting Your Documents in Order," you've got stuff all over the place. While the notebook technique enables you to consolidate all your financial matters physically, I would also ask you to simplify your finances structurally as well. For example:

- Direct-deposit Social Security and other monthly checks (i.e., dividends, annuities, pensions, etc.)

- Autopay as many bills as possible (e.g., utilities, memberships, church pledges, ongoing charity donations, etc.)

- Consolidate checking and savings account to one bank

- Transfer investment holdings, including IRAs, profit sharing, and 401(k)/403(b) accounts, to a single financial services company

Bottom line: The more you put on autopilot, the better off you will be as you move into your seventies, eighties, and beyond. For certain, the kid you designated your financial power of attorney will appreciate you for it.

Step Three: Transferring Roles between Spouses

In the preparations for discussing financial role reversal in the Other Talk, one area that often gets overlooked is the potential need to shift responsibilities from one spouse to another if one becomes incapacitated or dies.

Let's say one spouse has been handling the bill paying for most of their married life, and the other has been the hands-on investor as their nest egg began to grow. Clearly they need to give each other a quick tutorial on their respective areas of expertise.

- The bill payer should give a tour and possibly a road map of the payment process (e.g., autopay, e-mail, mail, etc.); the monthly budget, if it exists; and where receipts are kept.

- The investor should provide a detailed summary of what financial resources are available (which hopefully is housed in the Other Talk binder by now), and walk through the "what if" scenarios in the retirement income plan discussed earlier in this chapter.

Once they have given each other their respective orientations, the new designated bill payer and the new designated investor need to determine how much of that responsibility he or she is willing and able to take on. What often turns out to be a good solution is that the new designees will retain some of the responsibility, pass on parts of it to the kids, and turn over the rest to an outside expert.

Since these intraspousal determinations will have important implications for the kids, they should be made part of the Other Talk.

CHAPTER EIGHT

SELECTING THE MOST EFFECTIVE LIVING ARRANGEMENT

For most Americans, the desire to live in one's home throughout their last chapter is powerful and deep-seated:

- 90 percent of people older than sixty-five prefer to remain in their home, according to AARP.

- More poignantly, 90 percent of people, if they had less than six months to live, would choose limited care at home rather than advanced medical intervention in a hospital or nursing home, as reported in a recent Gallup poll.

This preference shouldn't be surprising, since there are a number of real benefits to living at home.

1. Spending your days in a familiar setting (perhaps where your children grew up, with the many pleasant memories that contains), surrounded by your "things" (family heirlooms, furniture and

other possessions that you bought with or for your spouse, kids' playthings and artwork).

2. Remaining near your friends and family, your social network, your neighborhood, your favorite stores and restaurants, and places of entertainment and worship.

3. Retaining feelings of independence, control, predictability, and self-esteem.

Then there's the flip side of this strongly held desire to live out your days at home, which is the gruesome image of the traditional alternative, the nursing home.

Many people think of it as a rather grim place where the residents shuffle about or sit in front of the television feeling bored, lonely, sad, and helpless.

For my great-uncle Virgil, it was the stark reminder of his mortality:

The only thing wrong with this place is that we're all old. We look around and are reminded of what we used to be and the things we can't do anymore. It's depressing.

For others, moving into a nursing home is often seen as a sign of failure, as observed by Elinor Ginzler, director of livable communities for AARP.

It means that they can no longer live independently, that they have diminished capabilities. Not surprisingly, many seniors go through a grieving process when deciding to move or when moving into an assisted-living facility.

It's the same sort of grief that one experiences with the loss of a loved one.

Perhaps the harshest, although often accurate, indictment comes from Dr. William Thomas, a leading proponent of nursing home reform, and creator of the Green House Project, which has redesigned the nursing home concept to give residents more privacy and more control over their lives:

I believe that in [nursing homes] in America, every year, thousands and thousands of people die of a broken heart. They die not so much because their organs fail, but because their grip on life has failed.

The reality is that many assisted-living facilities are much better than this dreary image. Further, new concepts have been and are being developed that go beyond the traditional "warehouse for the aging" approach.

One example is what is called a continuing-care retirement community (or CCRC), which provides various levels of health care at one location:

1. independent living, where you move into your own apartment when you are healthy and don't need personal assistance

2. assisted living, when you need a little help with the activities of daily living, like bathing and physical mobility

3. skilled nursing and rehabilitation, when round-the-clock monitoring and treatment are required

While this approach can prove beneficial for anyone in their last chapter, it is particularly appealing to couples, since it allows one spouse to receive a different level of care while allowing the two of them to continue socializing, dining, and being together.

Recipe for Disaster

But no matter how enlightened and homelike the facility, the most typical path to nursing home care is:

- The parent suffers a health crisis

- The family has forty-eight hours or less to explore options before the patient discharge

- The parent is placed into a nursing home without discussion

Because the decision to move the parent out of the house and into an institution occurred in the midst of a crisis, it's a recipe for disaster. As Sarah Wells, executive director of the National Citizens' Coalition for Nursing Home Reform, describes it:

It's a very emotional time when you're faced with a long-term care decision. It can be a time of chaos, often fast and furious.

Since there was no time to talk to and/or prepare the parent for the move, this short-term solution can easily morph into years of resentment and misery for parents and kids alike.

Making a Long-term Care Plan

My point is not to denigrate the value of nursing homes, CCRCs, or other forms of assisted-living facilities. For some people, the level of necessary care is far better than staying at home. For others, like my grandmother, it can be a liberating experience. Grandma, at age eighty, enthusiastically moved out of her house and into a continuing-care retirement community *primarily* for the wide range of social interactions and travel opportunities.

But to avoid your kids being swept up in the chaotic rush to the first nursing home available, you and your spouse need to make a long-term-care plan *now.* The two of you should have a thorough and realistic conversation about where you want to live in your last chapter, and how that can be accomplished. Then you'll want to make it an important component of the Other Talk, since your kids will surely be impacted, whether you settle on:

- living at home until the very end

- moving to some form of assisted living

- living with your kids

- or a combination of all of the above

As you prepare for this discussion, I would urge you to consider each of these four alternatives thoroughly and dispassionately, rather than emotionally embracing one and building a wall of defense against the other three.

Living at Home Until the Very End

It can be done.

I know, because my two brothers and I, living in different parts of the country, accomplished it for my parents, including the last seven years with Mom as a late-stage Alzheimer's patient and Dad struggling physically and mentally with multiple sclerosis.

It was emotionally draining, thoroughly exhausting, and incredibly time-consuming, mostly because we were making it up as we stumbled along. While at the end of the day we felt a sense of accomplishment in helping Mom and Dad achieve their passion, I know that a healthy dose of preplanning would have made this entire experience a whole lot better for everyone.

So that you can avoid some of our missteps, wrong turns, and dead ends, I will tell you how we would have done it differently, based on our own experience, plus my readings of and discussions with elder-care professionals.

1. Start with a realistic picture of living in your last chapter

I have already talked about the benefits of spending the rest of your days in your home:

- o familiar setting surrounded by your "things"

- o friends, family, neighborhood

- o independence, predictability, self-esteem

- o not to mention avoiding the dreaded nursing home

However, before succumbing to the emotional tug of the living-at-home option, you should honestly explore the challenges:

1. As you get older, you will need a hand with everyday tasks, like shopping and, eventually, transportation, cooking, bathing, etc.

2. As your health ultimately declines, you will need more and more access to health care.

3. As time goes on, the potential dangers of isolation and loneliness become more real, particularly for the physically and/or mentally handicapped.

You should also total up the obvious and not-so-obvious costs of living at home in your last chapter:

- o mortgage and/or home-equity loan payments

o   taxes and utilities, including projected increases

o   gas, maintenance, repairs, and insurance for an
    aging car(s) and aging drivers

o   public and/or private transportation

o   home maintenance and repair, since you
    eventually won't be doing it, if you ever did

If, after a thorough airing of the pros and cons, you decide
that living at home is best for you and your spouse, you
will want to take several steps to ensure that you will be
happy and secure in your decision.

2. Design your home of the future

The first step is to determine how to modify your home for
your later years of life, and how much it will cost. As a
result, you will not only be aware of the financial
implications of the necessary modifications, but you'll also
avoid the all-too-common strategy of, "I'll make those
changes after I fall and break my hip."

Of course, this careful evaluation of your surroundings is
important whether you elect to remain in your current
home, downsize to a more manageable property, or migrate
to another house in a different geography.

The basic concept in designing your home for your latter
years is called universal design, which means the user of

the space and his or her needs dictate the most effective layout of the living quarters. In your case, the goal is to maintain functional status as long as possible by focusing on:

comfort

accessibility

safety

Essentially, you will be modifying your home for decreasing mobility and sensory issues.

The good news is that while some of the changes—like moving the master bedroom and full bathroom to the first floor, or installing multilevel countertops in the kitchen and bathroom, or building an outdoor ramp—may prove costly, many of the alterations you can do yourself while you are still active, or have done for a modest cost.

In addition, if you are thinking about remodeling your home anytime in the future, you should incorporate universal design into your plans.

Here's a potpourri of basic adjustments to get you thinking about the kind of modifications you will want to include in your house of the future. Keep in mind that you don't have to perform all these adjustments at once, especially the wheelchair-accessible items, but you *should* have them in your plan. Finally, here's a suggestion to help you generate your own ideas: Borrow or rent a wheelchair for a day; then roll yourself around the house to get a different perspective on comfort, accessibility, and safety.

Throughout the house

1. lever-style door handles	easier to handle than doorknobs or when arms are full of packages
2. brighter lighting with adjustable controls	better for aging eyesight
3. handrails on both sides of all steps	easier to navigate
4. double-sided tape or carpet mesh to secure area rugs	avoid tripping or slipping
5. no threshold at entrance to the home	allows wheelchair occupant to enter with dignity and comfort
6. raised electrical outlets and lowered light switches	wheelchair accessible
7. strategically placed flashing light attached to doorbell	hearing impaired

Kitchen

1. under-cabinet lighting	better for aging eyesight
2. slide-out drawers	easier access to pots and pans
3. D-shaped cabinet and drawer handles versus knobs	easier to grasp

Bathroom

1. strategically placed grab bars in bath and shower (requires reinforcing spaces behind wall)	accessibility and safety
2. bath and shower chairs	comfort and convenience
3. lever handles on faucets	easier to handle
4. no floor barrier at shower entrance	accessibility

Professional Resources

There are a number of places to turn for help in evaluating your home and determining the most effective and cost-efficient ways to achieve comfort, accessibility, and safety in your home of the future. For example:

- – The National Association of Home Builders, in conjunction with the AARP, has developed a designated curriculum, Certified Aging-in-Place Specialist (CAPS) that trains remodelers how to design and implement home modifications for seniors.

- – There are hundreds of independent-living centers throughout the country that are nonprofit organizations that provide services to people with disabilities. Many offer free assessments of a home's architectural barriers, like steps and narrow doorways.

- A growing number of occupational therapists work with remodelers; many of them have undergone the CAPS training.

3. Prepare yourself for assisted living at home

Since you are currently physically active, mentally sharp, and in good health, now is the time to scope out extra help and services for when you're not, if you are serious about staying in your home. The key is to find good-quality and reliable sources of assistance at different levels of service. Below are a few places you may want to begin your search.

a. A home-health aide can provide a variety of nonmedical (but necessary) care, like doing housekeeping, buying groceries, preparing meals, doing the laundry, taking out the trash, getting you to the doctor, bathing and personal hygiene, taking you to a movie or a restaurant, or just sitting and sharing a conversation.

b. Adult day-care centers can provide an outlet for social interaction, mental stimulation, or just a place to hang out.

Fortunately, many of these places are beginning to recognize that, as Boomers become the new seniors, they "need to change the way they do business," according to Constance Todd, director of the National Institute of Senior Centers at the National Council on Aging. "That means salads instead of beef stew, theatrical productions instead of sing-alongs, fitness classes instead of bingo games, and computer seminars instead of knitting classes."

c. Geriatric-care managers can work with you and your family to create a personalized plan that integrates your medical care with your home care, as well as your financial and legal needs.

The geriatric-care manager then executes the plan by assigning and overseeing the necessary in-home support staff (e.g., nurses, social workers, exercise and nutritional specialists, and home-health aides), as well as collaborating with your doctors and medical specialists.

4. Explore funding opportunities as a home owner

Not surprisingly, the various assisted living services that will help keep you in your home as you age cost money. Hopefully, you have worked through your finances, as discussed in chapter seven, "Financing Your Uncertain Future," and will have (if you haven't already) taken the cost of these home-care services into account.

One advantage of staying in your home is that you have some unique opportunities to fund that lifestyle choice. Below are three possibilities that my brothers and I explored; there are certainly others that may better fit your situation. In any case, you will want financial and legal advice for whatever direction you decide to take.

a. Reverse mortgage

This financial instrument allows you to get your equity out without moving out of your home, and has become an increasingly popular choice, particularly as the Boomers start pouring into their retirement years.

Advantages

You qualify if you are sixty-two and you own your home free and clear, or owe a small enough amount that it can be paid off with part of your reverse-mortgage distribution. How much you can take out depends on your age and the value of the home, among other things.

You can take your equity out in a lump sum, as a monthly installment, or as a line of credit. The more you take out up front, the more you owe at the end, due to compounding interest.

If the value of your home declines, you will ultimately owe the lesser of the appraised value of the home or the amount of the outstanding loan.

Finally, you don't make any payments until you move out for more than a year (say, to an assisted-care facility), or vacate the premises either to another location or to the hereafter.

Disadvantages

The major drawback is the high up-front costs. Lenders can charge an origination fee (which can be as much as 2 percent of the loan) and mortgage insurance, as well as fees for appraisal, document preparation, recordation, escrow, title insurance, and brokerage, which can add up to as much as $10,000 to $12,000 on a $300,000 reverse mortgage.

In addition, these costs plus the monthly servicing and interest charges are all added to your outstanding loan. The result is that the amount owed grows over time, which, of course, is the reverse of paying off a traditional mortgage.

Further, interest rates can vary. You can get a fixed rate on a lump-sum distribution—great if rates are low. However, if you decide to go the monthly-installment or line-of-credit routes (which result in paying less interest than if you took the lump sum), the interest rate is variable.

It's also worth noting that, if you decide to keep the home in the family, your kids will have to pay the loan off in full if they ever decide to sell the house.

Finally, a reverse mortgage can adversely affect your eligibility for government assistance programs like Medicaid.

b. Line of credit

Another way to tap into your home equity without all the costs and machinations described above is a home-equity line of credit. This would cost little or nothing to set up. However, you should apply for this type of loan while you have a steady income that will convince the lender that you are a good credit risk.

Keep in mind that, unlike with the reverse mortgage, you will need to make regular monthly payments. But it is certainly a better option than paying high interest rates on credit card balances.

c. Medicaid waiver program

Another way to afford to stay in your home is to qualify for the Medicaid waiver program. Although every state doesn't offer this alternative, those that do help pay for health care services in your home versus a nursing home. Covered services may include case management, homemaker services, home-health aides, personal care, adult day programs, and respite care.

To qualify, you must meet the income and asset requirements in your state (which do not include the value of your home), as well as have a serious physical or mental condition. If you receive Medicaid services and you pass away, the state must try to recover the money it spent on your care from the estate.

Moving to Assisted Living Outside the Home

You should take the same disciplined, well-thought-out approach to this alternative as you did in considering the pros and cons of living in your home.

Further, by taking the initiative with your kids, whether it is for the traditional nursing home or the increasingly popular continuing-care retirement communities, which include independent living, assisted living, and nursing care, you will be inoculating your family against an all-too-common and destructive confrontation: dragging Mom and Dad out of their home and into a nursing home for their own good (or is it for your own peace of mind?).

By involving your kids in the discussion, as well as arranging family field trips to nearby facilities, you will be able to see for yourselves some of the advantages:

- common dining room

- transportation alternatives

- housekeeping

- activities meant to relieve isolation, loneliness, and boredom

- a la carte services for evolving personal care and medical needs

You should begin your research phase by checking the

quality ratings of your nearby facilities from independent sources like the federal government's Nursing Home Compare Web site.

Of course, when you make your actual on-site visits, you will want to go beyond just a look at the physical plant.

How does the staff approach their jobs?

Does the place feel like it's the residents' home, or is it a health-care institution?

Is it designed to make illness the center point of the residents' lives, or is it about life and living?

Are there lots of activities offered, or is the television in the dayroom the main focus?

In other words, how much of the place is "nursing" and how much is "home"?

Living with Your Kids

This living arrangement not only offers less expensive independent living for you and your spouse, but also can be a really positive experience for your kids and your grandchildren.

I remember spending my summers in a cottage in the middle of the woods in Michigan with my parents, brothers, and grandfather on my mother's side. Gramps, as we called him, brought a whole new dimension to my life, teaching me how to make a bow and arrow and how to track a deer, as well as regaling us all with tales of his growing up as a kid on the streets of London.

While living with your kids may sound good in the abstract, you will want the entire family to have a serious heart-to-heart discussion before you start packing your bags. Here are some questions that are designed to help you develop your own list of issues that you can lay out in the Other Talk.

- o What will be the financial arrangements?

- o What will be the costs of home renovation along the lines that were covered in the "Living at Home" section earlier in this chapter?

- o What are the expectations for babysitting, grocery shopping, housekeeping, etc.?

- o How will the kitchen be shared by multiple cooks?

- o How will you schedule time to sit down and share with one another how you think the arrangement is working out?

- o How will you keep your marriage relationship a high priority in your lives?

- o How can you remind your kids that they need to maintain the same priority with their spouses?

o How do your various children feel about your living with one of them?

o Should or could the living arrangement rotate among some or all of your children?

o What outside resources should you tap into for help in fulfilling your social needs and giving your kids a physical and psychological break from caregiving?

o How much will that cost?

o What happens if the arrangement doesn't work out?

o What happens if you become too sick or frail for your kids to handle?

o How will you as a group know that time has arrived?

Finally, whether this living arrangement is for you or not, I would suggest that you be careful how you approach this conversation with your kids. Several of my research respondents reported that their offspring were surprised and more than a little hurt when their parents declined to move in because they:

o didn't want to be a burden

o preferred being with people their own age

o didn't want to move away from their social
network

CHAPTER NINE

GETTING THE MEDICAL CARE YOU NEED

If you are the typical Baby Boomer, entering the world of retirement has never had so many positive dimensions. Compared to past generations, you are arriving with:

- a healthier physical condition, due to better nutrition and more attention to the importance of physical activity

- a longer average life expectancy: 83.5 for men, 84.8 for women (and that's just the average)

- more and better medical procedures and medications to keep you going strong as you cruise through your last chapter

But just as your ability to enjoy life, liberty, and the pursuit of happiness will be unprecedented in your retirement years, so are the challenges that you will face in getting adequate medical care.

As I pointed out in chapter four, "Navigating the Boomers' Perfect Storm," the rules of engagement will change in your last chapter.

- As you age, your need for resource-intensive health care will increase.

- The amount of public resources for your last chapter of life (e.g., Medicare, Medicaid, etc.) will most likely look vastly different than it does today.

- The availability of the traditional gatekeeper for your medical needs, the primary-care physician, is dwindling

- The number of fellow Boomers/elderly patients will increase exponentially, which will clearly put enormous strains on the current health-care delivery system.

Therefore, if you expect to get the medical care you need, you and your family should start *now* to develop an assertive, proactive, thoroughly researched, well-designed program to ensure access to an increasingly complex and constrained medical care system.

As you develop your Other Talk approach to the unique medical challenges of the Boomer generation, you should also keep in mind that it is already hard enough for senior citizens and their families to obtain the proper health care.

1. Lack of coordination

As you get older, chances are you will be treated by several different doctors, who may prescribe a variety of medications. The problem is that, for the vast majority of patients in the United States, there is no one medical practitioner who is charged with monitoring your condition or coordinating your various care providers. Here's how Dr. Gregg Warshaw, director of the Office of Geriatric and Family Medicine at the University of Cincinnati, describes the situation:

> *Individuals with three or four chronic illnesses have eight to fourteen physicians taking care of them. The complexity for caregivers is a tremendous challenge. Unfortunately, family physicians just aren't keeping track of all the specialists and medications a frail elder will need.*

2. Access to medical care

Trying to make sense of this complexity and chaos, even if you are one of the top experts on medical care for the elderly, like Dr. Robert Kane, can leave you frustrated and angry.

As reported in a National Public Radio interview, Dr. Kane tried for a couple of years to care for his elderly mother, who had had a stroke. But despite all his expertise, he couldn't get things to work.

> *My thirty years of practice and research weren't worth a dime. . . . If somebody with my experience*

and my knowledge couldn't make the system work,
what chance does the ordinary person have who
comes into this for the first time?

I don't know how it's going to play out in the
future, but I know right now we've got a mess on
our hands. We have a system that, quite frankly, is
broken; it's costing us a lot of money, and it isn't
producing the results that we'd like to see for
ourselves or our parents.

3. Conflicting, confusing choices

I heard on numerous occasions during my focus groups
with families that another extreme point of frustration is
trying to make medical decisions for yourself or for a
parent with imperfect information.

Greta, the daughter of a Parkinson's patient, described
her predicament this way:

> *The doctor says to me, "This is the decision you*
> *have to make. I can't make that decision for you."*

> *But if the doctor doesn't give you the information*
> *you need, how can he ever expect you to make a*
> *choice?*

Colleen, with tears rolling down her cheeks, added her
experience to the discussion:

> *In my mother's situation, there were two doctors*
> *on the team. One doctor said, "Don't take her off*
> *life support. She's got a chance."*

The other doctor, in the same room, said, "Take her off; nothing's going to help."

Well . . . what do I do?

4. Layers of trauma for your kids

Your kids can become pretty devastated in what can often be the cold, hard world of institutional medicine. This trauma is particularly likely if they are caught up in the middle of an unexpected parent-care crisis without the preparation and discussion from the Other Talk. Dr. Jerald Winakur, a practitioner of geriatric medicine for more than 30 years, paints this rather surreal picture:

> *The patient's family is already despondent, overwhelmed by Dad's (or Mom's) decline and the acute event that led to hospitalization (the pneumonia, the fall, the stroke); bewildered by his mental decline (the confusion, the weakness); frustrated in dealing with the hospital staff (the inattentive aides, the callous nurses, the harried attending physicians who often drift in and out like white-coated apparitions).*

5. Doctors' hidden agenda

In talking with a variety of medical practitioners and in researching the state of the profession, I was struck by the fact that the priorities doctors bring to their practices don't always include the patient.

First, doctors—and particularly primary-care

physicians—are under increasing pressure from insurance companies and Medicare to build patient volume (which may be why fewer of today's medical students are opting for primary care). This can be a particular problem for older patients, who may have more questions and need more detailed explanations. According to Dr. John Russo, an internist in West Orange, New Jersey:

> *My office visits are ludicrous; fifteen minutes and you're out. But economically you have to see so many more patients than you should just to keep the lights on. You can't sit and talk.*

A potential corollary to this economic burden is for doctors to recalibrate their practices based on profit margin. Today, the same medical care is reimbursed at different rates, depending on whether the doctor sees a patient with private insurance, Medicare, or Medicaid. As demand increases relative to supply, which is the essence of the Boomers' perfect storm, some doctors will be motivated to accept only patients whose coverage pays the higher rates.

Another observation about the doctors' agenda, particularly in the latter stages of the last chapter of life, is that doctors can become focused on cure at any cost, because they are trained to fix things. Why would smart, intelligent, hardworking people be so committed (in some cases obsessed) with "cure at any cost"? It's not only because of the mind-set established in medical school; it's also the amazing tools and techniques that they can now bring to bear.

Here's how Bernard, a social worker from my focus groups, characterized the situation:

> *What you've got are people who've always been the best of the best; they're very competitive to be successful; their goal is to always heal. . . . There are a lot of doctors out there where it's about them, and it's not about the patient and the family.*

Against this backdrop, I am heartened when I hear people like Leon Kass, a well-known physician and professor at the University of Chicago, take a much more profound look at the situation.

> *We need to remember that old age and dying are not problems to be solved, but rather human experiences to be faced.*

In fact, this is a fundamental tenet of the Other Talk.

6. You, as your own worst enemy

The final obstacle to getting the medical care you need could be you. Unfortunately, the denial and procrastination that so many people cling to as their last chapter unfolds can be particularly dangerous when applied to medical treatment.

In a *Wall Street Journal* article, "Tackling the Emotional Side of Cancer," writer Amy Dockser Marcus introduces Yvette, a larynx cancer patient, as a real-life example of the risk of rejecting reality.

Even when doctors told her that her prognosis was good, she said, "All I could hear was, 'You're going to die, you're going to die.'"

So she started breaking doctor's appointments because she was frightened by seeing other patients in the office who had trouble speaking because their voice boxes had been removed during treatment.

Preparing Yourself and Your Kids to Become Medical Advocates

I am not laying out these obstacles—the Boomers' perfect storm and the challenges of elder care—to scare or depress you. Rather, my goal is to inspire and motivate you to start the Other Talk process, because gone are the days when you could passively depend on the doctor to take care of things.

If you are to get the medical care you need, you and your kids will want to learn how to take control of your health care.

That means lining up the necessary resources *before* you need them, whether it's interviewing and selecting a geriatric doctor or geriatric-care manager, visiting retirement facilities and senior activity centers, or exploring the extent of funding opportunities from Medicare, long-term-care insurance, and beyond.

That means recognizing that the job of "medical advocate" is not only decision making on treatment options, living arrangements, living wills, etc. It is also coordinating various doctors and specialists, medical records, procedures, and current diagnoses, as well as negotiating with insurance companies, who are often the final arbiter over which treatment options will be covered.

That means that intimately involving your kids in your medical care not only lightens the load for you, but it also provides teaching moments for them when the time comes for them to do battle as geriatric patients.

To achieve these objectives, I recommend that you incorporate the following seven step checklist into your preparations for the Other Talk.

<u>Step One</u>
Talk with your spouse about which child or children would be the best candidate(s) for your medical power of attorney. As we did for your financial power of attorney, you should establish selection criteria for this function as well. For example, Linda Kaare, the elder-law attorney in Michigan, suggests someone who is:

- emotionally strong and courageous
- curious and a good communicator
- willing to challenge the doctor in a productive manner

As soon as your selected child has agreed to the responsibility and you have announced it to the family, you should sign the medical power of attorney document immediately. This is definitely a part of the Other Talk that you do not want to put off.

Step Two

Update the medical section of the notebook that I discussed in chapter six, "Getting Your Documents in Order." You will want to make sure that your medical history documentation is current. Then, as time goes on, you should begin to chronicle your proactive resource explorations, including doctor interviews, retirement home visits, medical record keeping, research into treatment options, etc.

In addition, I would recommend that you build a medical family history for both you and your spouse. The purpose is to create an understanding of potential risk factors by linking family genes to predisposition for many chronic illnesses, like heart disease and various forms of cancer.

The implication of these findings is not so you can live in fear and trepidation as you wait to be stricken by the "family curse." Rather, you can benefit on two levels:

1. Be proactive for conditions that are potentially preventable, including high blood pressure, heart disease, diabetes, depression, and alcoholism

2. Be on the lookout for early symptoms of diseases included in your family history, and begin to learn about treatment alternatives and emerging medical breakthroughs

According to a study published in the February 2012 issue of the *Annals of Internal Medicine*,

Detailed family information could help doctors better predict who is at risk and more accurately target patients for preventive care that may help avert the disease altogether.

It is also important to recognize when the risk of getting a disease is not necessarily heightened by family ties, as observed by Kelly Greene, the "Aging Well" columnist for *The Wall Street Journal.*

The genetic risk for Alzheimer's disease decreases dramatically between the ages of 60 and 85. . . . If you have a family member who contracted Alzheimer's after age 85, as many people do, there's little cause for worry.

In addition, I recommend that you review during your annual physical with your primary-care physician and/or gerontologist all your medications and specialist treatments.

> o Are they still effective in treating your current condition?

> o Are they still necessary and/or cost-effective?

Finally, I suggest that you explore the cost/benefits of routine screening for dementia, since it is estimated that 5 to 8 percent of people over the age of sixty-five have some form of dementia, and that that number doubles every five years over the age of sixty-five. This screening was controversial in early 2012, because the American College of Physicians, the U.S. Preventive Services Task Force, and the Alzheimer's Association discourage such regular monitoring, and recommend it be performed only if a patient reports a problem that could be due to dementia.

However, a study of eight thousand veterans aged seventy and older, reported in the February 2012 issue of the *Journal of Geriatrics Society,* indicated that

> *Proactive strategies such as routine screening are effective in diagnosing cognitive impairment . . . and have implications for strategies that seek to improve care and contain costs in dementia.*

Step Three

Take time to prepare for doctor visits with your child responsible for the medical power of attorney, whether he/she physically attends, participates via conference call or Skype, or is involved in before-and-after phone calls.

To get the most out of the limited time you have with the doctor during an office visit, and to overcome the intimidation factor of the doctor's white coat, you should create a set of questions that prioritize your concerns. Here are some suggestions from the Agency for Healthcare Research and Quality to get you started on your own list:

- What is my diagnosis?

- What are my treatment options? What are the benefits of each option? What are the side effects?

- Will I need a test? What is the test for? What will the results tell me?

- What will the medicine you are prescribing do? Are there any side effects?

- Why do I need surgery? Are there other ways to treat my condition? How often do you perform this surgery?

- Do I need to change my daily routine?

No matter what appears on your list, you don't want to save your most important or embarrassing question for the end, when the appointment is almost over, with little time to address your most pressing concern.

Step Four
Talk with your primary-care physician as you near sixty-five and become eligible for Medicare about his/her willingness to take you on as a Medicare patient. This is an important conversation to have, since doctor compensation is less for Medicare than with private insurance.

In preparation for your later years, you should also ask your doctor for recommendation/referrals for:

- A geriatric care manager who brings a working knowledge of health and psychology, human development, family dynamics, public and private resources, and funding sources to bear for you and your kids. The function of the GCM is to plan and coordinate health and psychological care, along with "living issues" like house modification, home care, socialization programs, and financial and legal planning.

- A geriatric doctor who is board certified in internal medicine or family practice but has undergone additional training to receive certification in geriatric medicine. The goal of this medical specialist is to prevent and treat diseases as they occur but also to manage your eventual decline, helping you to maintain independence and to age as well as possible.

Step Five

Seek out a second opinion when facing a major medical treatment, although be prepared for a potentially daunting task:

- Hospitals may put up major roadblocks because they see second opinions as time-consuming, distracting, and expensive.

- Doctors, especially specialists, may be resentful that their judgment is being questioned.

But second opinions are worth it nevertheless. In a Northwestern University review of 340 breast cancer patients seeking second opinions, reviewers disagreed with the first opinion 80 percent of the time, and altered mastectomy or lumpectomy plans for 8 percent of the women, as reported in *The New York Times*.

Step Six

Ensure that your medical care regimen includes an emphasis on preventive care, not just a focus on curing or treating an existing condition.

According to Daniel Perry, executive director of the Alliance for Aging Research,

> *Research shows that older patients aren't being steered toward the medical screening and preventive care they should get, even though Medicare would pay for much of it.*

> *Worse, there is a lot of withholding of aggressive treatment for older people, based not on the evidence of whether they will benefit but by the perception of the physician that they're too old to benefit.*

I can attest anecdotally from my focus groups to the validity of Mr. Perry's second assertion. Judson, a sixty-seven-year-old Parkinson's patient, related his experience when pressing his specialist about a clinical trial for a new experimental drug.

> *The young doctor just looked at me and said, "Sir, you don't get it. There is only a limited supply of the drug available. They aren't going to waste it on you."*

Step Seven

Be vigilant for developments that could have an impact on your health and well-being *and* help you stay afloat during the Boomers' Perfect Storm.

Certainly that means staying current on new drugs and

surgical techniques that could improve or sustain your condition. But it also means looking for ways to enhance the delivery of your medical care.

Below are three examples of delivery innovations that, at this writing, are beginning to garner serious interest. While they may or may not fit your pocketbook, I hope you find them instructive.

1. Home-health technology

    This concept enables doctors to check on patients with chronic but easy-to-monitor diseases (e.g., congestive heart failure, multiple sclerosis, diabetes, etc.) without requiring a physical face-to-face interaction. It's a device, installed in the home, that monitors symptoms on the spot and sends a report to the doctor (and family member, if desired) in real time.

    Benefits include fewer office visits, more productive and effective patient care, and a reduction in unnoticed complications that can result in hospitalization.

2. Patient-centered medical home model

    This concept is a health care delivery system that is currently being tested in a Medicare demonstration project. The basic approach is for the primary-care physician to take a more proactive role in your medical care, including:

        o managing and coordinating care

- o minimizing delays in getting appointments
- o partnering with patients with chronic diseases to manage their condition and prevent avoidable complications
- o provide nonurgent medical advice via e-mail and phone
- o offer a full spectrum of patient services from a team of health care professionals

It almost sounds like my childhood family doctor, except he also made house calls.

3. Concierge medicine

This concept, which initially emerged in the late nineties, is based on greater attention from your primary-care physician in return for an annual fee or retainer, which can vary widely from $600 to $5,000 per person.

Concierge doctors see fewer patients than a conventional practice, from a hundred to a thousand, versus the three to four thousand patients the average physician carries according to a June 2005 article in *Physicians Practice Journal.* Because of the lower caseload, concierge doctors offer more leisurely office visits, are available by cell phone or e-mail, and will schedule appointments within days rather than months.

* * * *

Navigating through the health care landscape during your last chapter of life will definitely be a challenge. But if you and your kids firmly commit to the advocacy approach to your medical care, I can assure you that your treatment outcomes will be better, your frustration level will be lower, and your children will be better schooled in managing their own health care.

CHAPTER TEN

TAKING CHARGE AT THE END OF YOUR LIFE

On the surface, this chapter heading could lead you to believe that my focus here is to help you ensure that decisions at the end of your life are made the way you want them to be. And, of course, it is.

But I also want you to go beneath the surface and realize that in most cases, it is not about *you* taking charge at the end of your life. It's about you preparing and empowering *your kids* to take charge as you approach that last sentence.

The reason for this collaborative approach is that it is highly likely that you won't be physically, emotionally, or mentally able to direct the final proceedings. It addresses the conundrum of how you will weigh options, make decisions, and articulate what ought to be done if you have lost cognitive clarity.

This is a very real problem, since, according to a recent Rand study, roughly 40 percent of deaths in the United States are preceded by a period of enfeeblement, debility, and often dementia lasting up to a decade.

As a result, it is critical that you start these conversations (as well as the rest of the Other Talk) *now*, while you are mentally sharp. Quite simply, the longer you wait the less effective these discussions with your kids will be, due to the natural deterioration of the aging brain. Here's how Branch Rickey, the legendary baseball general manager in the 1920s through the 1950s, describes that imperceptible evolution.

> *First, you forget names, then you forget faces, then you forget to zip up your fly, then you forget to unzip your fly.*

In preparing for the "end game" discussion in the Other Talk, there are three decision areas you will want to finalize.

Establishing guiding principles

The first step in making your kids confident and empowered in taking charge when the time comes is for you to confront and define what "being alive" means to you as you near the end.

For some people, it is fighting for every last breath: "Even one more day would be important to me; I would do everything I could to hold on to life."

For others, it is living intensely, yet comfortably, in the time remaining. "I would rather be able to do what I want, to be with my kids, to enjoy life, even if it's for a shorter time."

Of course, neither one is the better approach, because it is such a personal choice. But if you start now to build a clear understanding of your preferences with your family and your doctors, you can dramatically increase your odds of getting what you want.

Not surprisingly, coming to grips with what "being alive" means to you is easier said than done. Two tools that my wife and I have found helpful in confronting this issue (and which are available online) are:

- "Five Wishes," developed by Aging with Dignity, which is a booklet that you fill out to help you articulate your feelings and opinions about:

    1. the person you want to make care decisions for you when you can't

    2. the kind of medical treatment you want or don't want

    3. how comfortable you want to be

    4. how you want people to treat you

    5. what you want your loved ones to know

- "The Proxy Quiz for Family or Physician," created by the ABA Commission on Law and Aging, which is a set of ten questions about your personal medical preferences, which you, your kids, and your doctor fill out separately. You then compare answers to find out where you need to correct the perceptions of your kids and/or your doctor on how you want to be treated at the end of your life

One thing is certain: If you elect to procrastinate defining what "being alive" means to you, and fail to empower your kids to achieve it, you will find yourself in the clutches of the medical profession's default position of treatment until cured (or dead).

There are a number of reasons for the medical profession's mind-set.

1. Medical technology allows today's doctors to bring a dizzying array of medications and techniques to the table. Robert, one of my focus group respondents with ten years as director of medicine at a major Chicago hospital, painted this "because we can" scenario:

    There is always another layer of hope that we've created in medicine. We've got so many alternatives.

    If you don't have to pay for it and if there is no downside, you don't want Mom to miss an opportunity to continue living.

2. A corollary to the power of technology is that it can cloud medical judgments. Victor, another one of my doctor respondents, described the moral dilemma this way:

Thanks to medicine's prowess in sustaining life, it is harder than ever to know when to stop.

And because we as doctors are trained to "find the cure," we often forget to ask ourselves, "Is the illness getting the attention, or is the patient getting the attention?"

3. Medicare is set up to fund treatment until cured. It's the reason that more than 25 percent of all Medicare spending is for the 5 percent of patients who are in the final year of life.

   The cause, according to Muriel Gillick, a geriatrics expert at Harvard Medical School, is *that the way Medicare is organized encourages too many interventions toward the end of life that may extend the patient's life span only slightly, if at all, and can cause unnecessary suffering. It would often be better not to try so hard to eke out a few more hours or weeks, but rather to concentrate on quality of life.*

4. We have been convinced by popular culture of the omnipotence of medical technology. In a study of a full season of medical shows like *ER,*

   - 75 percent of patients who received CPR during cardiac arrest survived
   - 67 percent recovered enough to leave the hospital

   In reality, a 2010 study of more than ninety-five

thousand cases of CPR found that only 8 percent of patients survived for more than a month. Of these, only 3 percent could return to a normal life.

5. The upshot is that, while the doctor is busy trying to fix the problem, the patient as a human being can get lost in the shuffle.

    – "We're prolonging life but we're also prolonging dying," observes Mercedes Bern-Klug, an end-of-life researcher at the University of Iowa. "Hundreds of thousands of people are surviving longer with advanced dementia or traumatic brain injuries or in coma states.

    In addition, for their loved ones, coping with the ambiguity of 'not quite dead' creates a whole other level of stress."

    – Nadia, one of my doctor respondents who was practicing in the United States on a fellowship, described her utter disbelief at how dying patients are treated in our society.

    Everybody is treated until they are dead. Even if they are semi dead, they are still treated. The patients are laying there at age ninety-five, ninety-six, one hundred, debilitated, demented, don't recognize anyone, don't eat, don't pee. They're still treated.

6. Perhaps best capturing the emotional angst that can be visited on your kids by the medical community is Lester, a 58 year old care-giving son.

> *My father was at a very advanced stage of Alzheimer's. But the doctors kept hounding me; they would call me at work three or four times a week, telling me, "You shouldn't send him back to the nursing home; you should leave him in the hospital."*

> *The fact is, the decision had been made a year ago with a health care power of attorney. It was very emotionally trying for me. I knew he was going to die shortly. But they made me feel, "If you take him out of the hospital, you are the one who is causing his death."*

Setting your parameters for medical treatment

Step two in taking charge of your life (versus abdicating it to the medical community) is to put your preferences in writing. Equally important is to distribute and discuss your wishes with your family members and your doctors to ensure that your goals will be achieved.

An effective and relatively inexpensive way to accomplish this is to consult with your legal adviser, then draw up a health care power of attorney.

This document establishes your designated agent who will make health care decisions for you if you are not able to do so. While rules can vary by state, typically responsibilities include the power to require, consent to, or withdraw any type of personal care or medical treatment, and to admit you to or discharge you from any hospital, nursing home, or other institution.

A specific statement is included that allows you to address your opinion on life-sustaining treatment. For demonstration purposes only, here is the language for the three choices from the Illinois statutory short-form power of attorney for health care:

- I do not want my life to be prolonged nor do I want life-sustaining treatment to be provided or continued if my agent believes the burdens of the treatment outweigh the expected benefits. I want my agent to consider the relief of suffering, the expense involved and the quality as well as the possible extension of my life in making decisions concerning life-sustaining treatment.

- I want my life to be prolonged and I want life-sustaining treatment to be provided or continued unless I am in a coma which my attending physician believes to be irreversible, in accordance with reasonable medical standards at the time of reference. If and when I have suffered irreversible coma, I want life-sustaining treatment to be withheld or discontinued.

- I want my life to be prolonged to the greatest extent possible without regard to my condition, the chances I have for recovery or the cost of the procedures.

If you are in the "do not prolong life at any cost" camp, you will also want to explore these two health care directives:

1. The living will establishes that you do not want your death to be artificially postponed. It states that if your attending physician determines that you have an incurable injury, disease, or illness:

    - procedures that only prolong the dying process should be withheld or withdrawn

    - only the administration of medication, sustenance, or surgical treatments (as determined by your attending physician) that provide comfort care should be used

    This document must be signed by two witnesses who will not benefit from your death.

2. The Do Not Resuscitate (DNR) order is different from the health care power of attorney and the living will in that you or your health care agent cannot prepare it. Rather, it is a written order signed by your physician that instructs other health care providers not to attempt CPR if your heart has stopped beating and if you have stopped breathing during cardiac or respiratory arrest.

Since it is often relevant during an emergency situation, it is advisable to carry a DNR card, as well as to distribute the document to family members and your doctors.

Once you have distributed your "what being alive means to me" documents (the health care power of attorney and, if relevant, the living will and the DNR order) and thoroughly discussed them during the Other Talk, you and your family should acknowledge the possibility of revisions. Every time your health status changes in some significant way, you should have another discussion to clarify your views and expectations.

It is okay for you to move the goalposts on issues pertaining to the end of your life. You just need to make certain that the people in your world know that you have moved them.

Taking the hospice exit

The final area for your consideration is to consider the pros and cons of hospice.

Because of the starting point in the hospice process, giving up medical treatment, this option at the end of life isn't for everyone, certainly not for those who want to battle until their last breath. For you to qualify for Medicare coverage of hospice, at least one doctor must certify that you have six months or less to live and have agreed to forgo life-prolonging treatments like dialysis, chemotherapy, and radiation.

The essence of hospice is that it isn't about perpetuating life; it is about perpetuating quality of life.

Conventional health care generally believes that when there is no possibility of recovery, the job is complete.

Hospice, on the other hand, believes that as long as a person continues to live, a great deal can be done:

- keeping the patient as comfortable as possible

- supporting the family as much as possible

- making the quality of life as fulfilling as possible

- for as long as possible

It achieves this by medically controlling a patient's pain and symptoms, and, with psychologist and social workers, by helping him or her grapple with depression, anxiety, fear, and spiritual issues. In addition, patients are encouraged to talk about feelings toward family members, regrets, and fences that may need to be mended.

Equally important, hospice treats family members as part of the plan for care.

- Nurses visit once a week (or more frequently as needed) and are on call twenty-four/seven to respond to crises and questions on the phone or in person.

- Social workers visit as often as necessary to provide emotional support, as well as find resources for wills, power of attorney, funeral plans, etc.

- Home health aides assist with bathing, personal care, and homemaking to relieve family caregivers so they can take a break.

- Bereavement counselors provide care to the family for up to a year after the patient's death.

Jacques, one of my internist respondents, painted the picture of hospice this way:

It's about not suffering. It's about dignity and control and respect. It's about being able to go home, where you can just be comfortable with pain medicine and oxygen and not be in a hospital.

What may surprise you (it certainly amazed me) is that hospice care doesn't shorten your life span, even though the hospice patient stops hospital treatments and is permitted high-dose narcotics to combat pain. In fact, in a study of nearly forty-five hundred terminally ill Medicare patients, those who received hospice care lasted longer than those who didn't:

- Pancreatic cancer patients lived an extra three weeks

- Lung cancer patients lived an additional six weeks

- Congestive heart failure patients lived an extra three months

How is this possible? Perhaps you live longer only when you stop trying to live longer. You are able to spend the remaining time at home, surrounded by your stuff, taking the opportunity to prepare yourself and your kids for the last sentence. You have an uninterrupted space to reminisce, talk about unresolved issues, and say your good-byes to family and friends in a familiar, comfortable, pain-free setting.

CHAPTER ELEVEN

BEING THERE FOR YOUR KIDS

Fight to the end or achieve a comfortable departure.

It is one of the most important decisions you will ever make.

It is also one of the most courageous because you are taking the initiative to consider how you want your last sentence to be written.

Woody Allen once said,

I'm not afraid of dying.
I just don't want to be there when it happens.

But because you have committed to having the Other Talk, you have decided that you **do** want to be there when it happens.

Because you want to be there for your kids.

On the surface, the Other Talk sounds like it is about being a great parent, about preparing your kids for one of life's great challenges. And it is.

But it also carries with it the added value of freeing you and your family to focus on getting the most out of the rest of your time together.

Finally, it works to help ensure your family's well-being, financially and emotionally, when you are gone.

In essence, the Other Talk will be an important part of your legacy.

Your kids will love you for it!

Appendix

ONLINE RESOURCES TO HELP CREATE A BETTER OTHER TALK

To help you develop your knowledge base, fill in your Other Talk notebooks (either paper or electronic) for each of your kids, and begin to explore your options for the four facts of life:

1. Financing your uncertain future

2. Selecting the most effective living arrangement

3. Getting the medical care you need

4. Taking charge at the end of your life

I have built a sampling of informative Web sites that are organized around each of the action chapters, five through ten. The number of these sites, both for-profit and nonprofit, can be expected to grow as the interest in these subjects, particularly among Boomers and their families, mushrooms.

Because these Web sites are real-time resources, they will help you stay on top of your options, emerging medical treatments, and changing legal and financial regulations.

Finally, I would be interested in your feedback on the usefulness of these Web sites, as well as any additions you feel we should make. You can reach me at tim.prosch@ theothertalk.com.

Chapter Five: Setting the Stage for the Other Talk

Benefits Checkup from the National Council on Aging *(*www.benefitscheckup.org*)*

> Helps you find federal, state, local and private benefit programs for which you may be eligible

*National Council on Aging (*www.ncoa.org*)*

> Provides you with information on economic and health issues for seniors

*National Aging in Place Council (*www.ageinplace.org*)*

> Provides information on financial and caregiving options to help you to stay in your own home

*Area Agency on Aging (*www.n4a.org*)*

> You can search a database of state and local chapters that provide a variety of supportive services, including help with household chores, meals served in community locations, adult day care programs, protective services, and legal counseling.

National Highway and Transportation Safety Association *(*www.nhtsa.gov*)*

> Search for "Driving Safely while Aging Gracefully" for a checklist to see whether you should still be driving

*Transportation for Seniors (*www.kued.org*)*

> Search for "Community Transportation Resource Worksheet" provides a worksheet to help you determine what transportation needs can be met by

your community resources and public transportation.

Association for Driver Rehabilitation Specialists (www.driver-ed.org)

Helps you find a certified driving therapist who can help you determine whether it's time to give up driving, and can also help you retrofit your vehicle if you have lost certain mobility

AARP (www.aarp.org)

Membership organization for people fifty and older, providing a variety of age-specific products and services

FBI's Task Forces on seniors (www.fbi.gov/scams-safety/fraud/seniors)

Helps you determine whether you are being defrauded by unscrupulous people

Women's Institute for Secure Retirement (www.wiserwomen.org)

Provides tools to improve long-term financial security for women

Strength for Caring (www.strengthforcaring.com)

Provides you with access to others dealing with aging issues through "Share your Story" and "Meet Other Caregivers" online bulletin boards

Chapter Six: Getting Your Documents in Order

*Lotsa Helping Hands (*www.lotsahelpinghands.com.com*)*

> You can upload and share your schedule with family and friends, and you can indicate areas where you need help. Also provides you with financial, legal, and medical documents, and discussions with relevant experts

*National Academy of Elder Law Attorneys (*www.naela.org*)*

> Provides you with information on how and why an elder law attorney can help in the areas of healthcare, retirement, tax and financial/estate planning. You can search the database to find an elder law attorney to assist in estate and Medicaid planning

*"Do Not Call" list (*www.donotcall.gov*)*

> List your phone number so you can get off unwanted mailing and calling lists

*ABA Commission on Law and Aging (*www.american bar.org*)*

> Search "Proxy" to find a quiz for your family and or doctor to determine your wishes for medical treatment toward the end of life. Provides you with information on scams against seniors

*Aging with Dignity (*www.agingwithdignity.org*)*

> You can fill out the "Five Wishes" document,

which helps you express how you want to be treated if you are seriously ill and unable to speak for yourself

Do Not Resuscitate (www.help4seniors.org)

Search "POLST—Physicians Order for Life-sustaining Treatment." POLST converts your wishes regarding resuscitation into a formal medical order to be discussed with your doctor while you are still in good mental acuity, and should be kept in your doctor's medical records

Important Records (www.archives.com)

Provides access to your birth, death, and marriage and divorce records for a fee

Chapter Seven: Financing Your Uncertain Future

*AARP (*www.aarp.org*)*

Search "4 Ways to Tap Your House for Cash"

*The National Reverse Mortgage Lenders Association (*www.reversemortgage.org*)*

Free publications to help you determine whether a reverse mortgage is right for you

*NCOA Home Equity Advisor (*www.homeequityadvisor.org*)*

Information on reverse mortgages and consumer protections

*National Center for Home Equity Conversion (*www.reverse.org*)*

Information on how you can get a reverse mortgage and how to use the proceeds for long-term-care expenses, insurance premiums, or purchasing a less expensive primary residence

*North American Securities Administrators Association (*www.nasaa.org/investor-education*)*

Provides tools and techniques on what to watch for and what to do if you think you are being scammed by financial advisers

*The Financial Planning Association (*www.fpanet.org*)*

You can search a database to find a financial planner

*National Association of Personal Financial Advisors (*www.napafa.org*)*

You can search a database of financial advisers. Also provides tips and techniques on financial planning

*Elder Financial Protection Network (*www.bewiseonline.org*)*

Provides information on ways to protect yourself from online scams

Chapter Eight: Selecting the Most Effective Living Arrangement

*National Alliance for Caregiving (*www.caregiving.org*)*

Provides you with a clearinghouse of resources for seniors that have been reviewed and rated

*Nursing homes, home health, and hospitals (*www.medicare.gov/nhcompare*)*

You can search a database that compares nursing homes, home health care providers and hospitals in your area

*National Care Planning Council (*www.longtermcarelink.org*)*

You will find links to all types of senior care services and a directory to find local organizations

*LeadingAge (*www.leadingage.org*)*

You can search a database of nursing homes, home health care providers, hospitals and community services for seniors (does not provide comparisons)

*Home Safety Council (*www.homesafetycouncil.org*)*

Provides information on how you can reduce injuries

*The National Resource Center on Supportive Housing and Home Modification (*www.homemods.org*)*

You can search a database of hundreds of resources

for home modification in your area. Offers tips on how to assess your home safety and tells you about funding sources for home modification

*National Association of Home Builders (*www.nahb.org*)*

Offers information on how to modify your home and how to find a certified professional who specializes in aging-in-place remodeling

*American Society of Interior Designers (*www.asid.org*)*

Provides you with information about "universal design," which is meant to produce buildings, products, and environments that are inherently accessible to both people without disabilities and people with disabilities

*The Center for Universal Design (*www.design.ncsu.edu/ cud*)*

Information about improving accessibility in your home

*Eldercare Locator (*www.eldercare.gov*)*

Finds government services and programs in your area that are designed for senior citizens

*Meals on Wheels (*www.MealCall.org*)*

You can find a local provider of nutritious frozen prepared meals that can be delivered to your home

*National Aging in Place Council (*www.ageinplace.org*)*

You can search a database of service providers that can help you stay in your home. Also provides advice for ways for you to stay at home

Center for Aging Services Technology (www.agingtech. org)

Provides you with information on aging-in-place technology

Cohousing Association of America (www.cohousing.org)

You can determine where cohousing groups exist in your area or how to start your own cohousing community

National Adult Day Services Association (www.nadsa.org)

Provides information on how to choose an adult day center and a database to help find a center in your area

National Association of Professional Geriatric Care Managers (www.caremanager.org)

You can find a geriatric care manager in your local community. Provides an explanation of the duties and responsibilities of a geriatric care manager

Nursing homes without walls (www.pace4you.org)

You can search a database to find a local PACE program that provides you with one stop shopping for all the services you might need to remain in your home

National Association for Home Care and Hospice
(www.nahc.org)

You can search a database to find local home care and hospice agencies

Gay Retirement Guide (www.gayretirementguide.com)

Information on gay/lesbian retirement communities

National Center for Assisted Living (www.ahca.org)

You can learn how to choose an assisted-care facility

National Consumers League (www.natlconsumersleague. org)

Provides you with information on frauds and scams

Assisted Living Federation of America (www.alfa.org)

You can find an assisted-living community in your local area. Provides a checklist to help you assess services, amenities, and accommodations

National Association of Realtors
(www.seniorsrealestate.com)

You can find a local Realtor who specializes in selling homes of seniors going through major lifestyle transitions

Chapter Nine: Getting the Medical Care You Need

The Family Navigator (www.caregiver.org)

> You can find information on caring for a loved one, including a handbook for long-distance caregivers

eCare Diary (www.ecarediary.com)

> You can share an online calendar so family, friends, and community can determine how and when they can help out. Also provides links for legal documents by state

CareFlash (www.careflash.com)

> Provides a system for a private online calendar so family, friends, and community can determine how and when they can help

Medicare Rights (www.medicarerights.org)

> Provides an independent source for you to learn about health care assistance for people with Medicare

American Geriatrics Society (www.healthinaging.org)

> Provides you with health information about diseases that are prevalent in older adults

Hospital Quality Alliance (www.hospitalqualityalliance. org)

> You can easily compare hospitals in your area on quality measures based on patient surveys

National Council on Patient Information and Education
    *(*www.talkaboutrx.org*)*

> You can learn the appropriate use of your
> medications, how they might affect you as you age,
> and how to better manage them

American Society of Consultant Pharmacists
    *(*www.ascp.com*)*

> You can find a senior care pharmacist in your
> community who can help you manage your
> medications

*Patient Advocate Foundation (*www.patientadvocate.org*)*

> You can learn how to appeal insurance company
> denials of coverage and discrimination because of
> an illness

*Alzheimer's Association (*www.alz.org*)*

> You can learn more about the medical and
> emotional issues surrounding Alzheimer's

*National Institute on Aging (*www.nia.nih.gov*)*

> You can find information on senior health topics,
> with an emphasis on Alzheimer's

*American Heart Association (*www.heart.org*)*

> You can learn more about the medical and
> emotional issues surrounding heart conditions

*American Cancer Society (*www.cancer.org*)*

> You can learn more about the medical and emotional issues surrounding cancer

*National Comprehensive Cancer Network (*www.nccn.org*)*

> Provides you with ways to cope with distress, including meditation, keeping a journal, joining a support group, and creating a support team of family and friends

*Leukemia and Lymphoma Society (*www.lls.org*)*

> Offers help for asking doctors questions and understanding the answers with their "Toolkit for Older Adults with Cancer and their Caregivers"

There are many more sites for diseases prevalent among seniors.

Chapter Ten: Taking Charge at the End of Your Life

National Hospice and Palliative Care Organization
*(*www.nhpco.org*)*

> You can learn more about end-of-life issues and download state-specific advance directives

National Center on Elder Abuse
*(*www.elderabusecenter.org*)*

> You can learn how to protect yourself if you feel you are being taken advantage of by a family member(s)

National Hospice and Palliative Care Organization
*(*www.caringinfo.org*)*

> You can learn more about end-of-life issues

*National Funeral Directors Association (*www.nfda.org*)*

> You can learn more about traditional funerals, cremation, and dealing with grief

*The Funeral Consumers Alliance (*www.funerals.org*)*

> You can learn from an independent source how to plan a funeral and how to make sure that your legal rights as a consumer are respected. Also provides information on green burials

*Americans for Better Care of the Dying (*www.abcd-caring.org*)*

> You can learn more about end-of-life issues,

including the aptly titled "Handbook for Mortals"

Hospice Foundation of America
(www.hospicefoundation.org)

You can learn more about the hospice concept of care, as well as suggestions for dealing with grief in workplaces, schools, and places of worship

Hospice Care (www.caringinfo.org)

Learn more about hospice and palliative care, as well as find options in your community

National Institute for Jewish Hospice (www.nijh.org)

You can learn more about specific issues surrounding hospice for those of the Jewish faith. You can also find accredited Jewish hospitals and hospice organizations

Islamic Medical Association of North America
(www.imana.org)

You obtain an advance directive that balances Islamic prohibitions against suicide with the desire to not prolong life at all costs

American Bar Association (www.americanbar.org)

Consumer's tool kit for healthcare advance planning is an excellent set of questions to start your conversation about healthcare directives

TIM PROSCH

WORK SHEET TEMPLATE FOR THE OTHER TALK

To help you organize all the information and documentation that you will want to include in your Other Talk notebooks (which, of course, can be electronic rather than a physical binder,) I have created a template that you can adapt to focus your efforts.

My goal here is to lay out the task in bite size pieces for each of the action chapters rather than present you with one large, overwhelming project.

So, whether you decide to divvy up specific assignments by family member or do it all yourself, you will have a running checklist on the issues, information and discussions that you are ready for and those that still need to be worked on.

Finally, please keep uppermost in your mind that the Other Talk is about enhancing relationships and sharing responsibilities with your kids rather than just an exercise in collecting paperwork for a notebook.

Chapter Five: Setting the Stage for the Other Talk

Start with your commitment to the philosophy of the Other Talk

- Acknowledge the inevitability of ceding the decision making and management of your day-to-day responsibilities to your kids

- Establish ground rules on the trigger points that will effect the change of responsibilities in key functions, such as bill paying, transportation, living arrangements, money and asset management, and medical decisions

- Realize that your plan for role reversal is not about the loss of power and control but rather the gain of security and freedom

- Incorporate full financial disclosure into the partnership with your kids

Prepare your kids emotionally and psychologically

- Consider giving each of your kids a copy of this book before you sit down to have the Other Talk

- Encourage your kids to adopt the collaborative mindset that is inherent in the Other Talk with you and their siblings

Establish that the Other Talk is an on-going annual

conversation, not a one-time event, to allow the family to deal with changes in your physical, mental and financial condition as well as external factors (e.g. medical breakthroughs, government policy revisions, etc.)

Spend time creating a welcoming and engaging environment for the Other Talk.

Chapter Six: Getting your Documents in Order

In preparation for the Other Talk, you need to collate and organize binders (either electronic or paper) for each of your kids that will not only give them a working knowledge of your situation and your philosophies but also will house a knowledge base that can be updated as time goes on.

1. The Will

    - location of original document
    - date last revised

2. Medical

    Copies of advanced directives (health care power of attorney, living will and DNR)

    Information on doctor(s)

    - name and contact information
    - medical specialty
    - brief description of diagnosis
    - treatment plan and timeline

    Summary of medications

    - type and strength of prescription
    - what the medication is treating
    - location for prescription refills (pharmacy or mail order)
    - physician who wrote the prescription

3. Financial

   Contact information for key advisors (i.e. attorney, financial planner, accountant, stockbroker, real estate agent, etc.) including name, address, phone and fax numbers and email address

4. Key documents

   Location of the original for the following:

   - birth certificate
   - Social Security card
   - marriage certificate
   - if applicable, divorce judgment and decree, or the stipulation agreement if settled out of court
   - passport
   - trust documents

5. Insurance for life, health, home(s), vehicles and boats

   Name of the carrier, the policy number, policy type, and the agent connected with each policy

6. Location of your most recent seven years of tax returns

7. Location, account numbers and contact information for each of your checking and savings accounts as well as the location and contents of your safety deposit box

8. Proof of ownership

   Location of original documents for housing and land ownership deeds

- cemetery plots
- vehicle and boat titles
- savings bonds
- partnership or corporate operating agreements

9. Location of investment, pension and loan information

- inventory of current investments, including taxable and traditional and Roth IRA accounts, 401K and 403b, plus the account numbers and the contact information for who handles each

- your latest statement from Social Security

- original mortgage and any home equity loans and most recent refinancing details

- summary of loans you have outstanding and the repayment terms

- summary of debts you owe

10. Credit card information

Location of most recent statement plus front-and-back copies of all active credit cards

11. Burial and Funeral

Summary of your wishes on:

- cremation or burial

- type of service (where, what kind, visitation, specific music and/or readings, military proceedings, etc.)

- organ donation arrangements and time frame

- location of burial plot, type of grave marker

- charity donation in lieu of flowers

Prepaid funeral/burial insurance

Name of the carrier, the policy number, policy type and specifics, and the agent connected with policy

Chapter Seven: Financing your uncertain future

Frame your spending priorities by answering the question:

*What is the life you want, what is the life you don't want
and what are the costs of each?*

Establish goals and priorities by decade: sixties, seventies, eighties, nineties

Develop a retirement income plan which will require you to accumulate the following information

Annual expenses

- essential expenses

- discretionary expenses (e.g. travel, entertainment, clothes, etc.)

- supplemental health care insurance

- long term health care insurance

Income

- Social Security benefits and start dates for husband and for wife

- pension benefits

- annuity income

- other income (e.g. dividends, interest, rental income, real estate sale including your home, etc.)

Current assets

- investment portfolio, including the dollar amount and percentage of total for stocks, bonds and short-term instruments

- real estate and other assets (e.g. antiques, artwork, etc.)

- level of risk you are comfortable with

Answer key decisions in your retirement plan (the free financial planning software programs can be helpful)

1. How long will you and your spouse live?

2. Can your investment portfolio at least match the rate of inflation?

3. Have you established a withdrawal rate that won't jeopardize your long-term future?

4. Have you set aside funds to supplement Medicare and cover out-of-pocket health care costs?

5. Do you want to leave an inheritance for your kids and others as well as donations to charity or do you plan to spend it all?

Establish a financial power of attorney with one of your kids

Schedule time for you and all your kids to sit down for face-to-face meetings with you and any financial advisors you might have (e.g. banker, lawyer, broker, accountant, insurance agent, financial planner, etc.)

Prepare now for potentially shifting financial roles between you and your spouse

Chapter Eight: Selecting the most effective living arrangement

In preparation for the Other Talk, thoroughly discuss with your spouse where you want to live in your last chapter and how that can be accomplished

- Living at home until the very end

- Moving to some form of assisted living

- Living with your kids

- or a combination of all of the above

Living at home until the very end

- including help with everyday tasks, more frequent access to health care, and potential loneliness and isolation as well as the various costs of home ownership

- prepare to modify your home to maximize comfort, accessibility and safety

- start now to educate you and your family about assisted living at home alternatives

- explore funding opportunities as a homeowner including reverse mortgage, line of credit, Medicaid waiver program, etc.

Moving to an assisted living facility

- arrange family field trips to nearby facilities to evaluate the pros, cons and costs of various alternatives

- evaluate each facility to determine how much of the place is "nursing" and how much is "home"

Living with your kids

- initiate a serious heart-to-heart discussion on the various emotional, physical and financial implications

Chapter Nine: Getting the medical care you need

Recognize that obtaining quality health care as a geriatric patient will likely be more complicated, confusing and frustrating than when you were younger

As you sail into the Boomers' Perfect Storm, prepare yourself and your kids to become medical advocates

- Designate one of your kids as medical power of attorney

- Ensure that your medical history documentation is current

- Take time to prepare for doctor visits with your child responsible for the medical power of attorney

- Discuss with your doctor how your relationship may change once you become eligible for Medicare

Chapter Ten: Taking charge at the end of your life

Establish guiding principles with family *and* doctors

- Define what "being alive" means to you

- Consider using tools to help you and your kids get through this most difficult of conversations (e.g. Five Wishes, Proxy Quiz for Family or Physician, etc.)

Set your parameters for end-of-life medical treatment with medical power of attorney, living will and Do Not Resuscitate, if appropriate

Consider the pros and cons of hospice

ABOUT THE AUTHOR

Throughout my career, I have focused my energies and attention on understanding and addressing the needs, wants and challenges of the Baby Boom generation for a variety of national and international organizations.

For the past 15 years, I have homed in on elder care and end of life issues.

That experience combined with four specific events drove me to write this book:

1. Over the last ten years, I have been interviewing hundreds of Baby Boomers to determine the perceptions, attitudes and mindset that this unique generation brings to the various decisions at the end of life. One clear message is that Boomers do not want their kids to suffer through the same frustrations, arguments and unpleasant surprises that they experienced in their parents' last chapter of life.

2. In 2005, the Terri Schiavo case captured the attention (and heartstrings) of the world, especially the tug of war between Terri's husband and her parents over what she wanted done at the end of her life.

3. Concurrently, over the last five years, I have experienced, through the rapidly declining health of my own parents, the escalating frustrations and financial crises that lack of communication can create.

4. Finally, for the Baby Boomers, there is a Perfect Storm that has been brewing in geriatric care in recent years and it's scheduled to hit the Boomers just as they reach 65.

   - More: 65+ population will grow 60% between now and 2025

   - Longer: Today's 65 year old will live for another 18.5 years

   - Fewer: Supply of primary care physicians as well as geriatric doctors and nurses is declining

Boomers and their families need to start preparing. They should start having the Other Talk *now*, then keep on talking.

This book is the catalyst that can get you there!

THE OTHER TALK

CPSIA information can be obtained at www.ICGtesting.com
Printed in the USA
LVOW131113301212

313763LV00002B/212/P